NOW IS THE TIME:

INTEGRATION IN THE BERKELEY SCHOOLS

INTEGRATION IN THE

b y

Now Is The Time:

BERKELEY SCHOOLS

NEIL V. SULLIVAN

WITH *Evelyn S. Stewart*

FOREWORD BY MARTIN LUTHER KING, JR.

Indiana University Press

BLOOMINGTON / LONDON

To the tens of thousands of berkeley people—
adults and children—who are making school integration a reality.

ACKNOWLEDGMENTS

Without the help of many persons, this book would not exist. Specifically, I want to thank these friends and colleagues: Thomas Wogaman, formerly my administrative assistant, who read the manuscript for factual accuracy; Daniel Freudenthal, who read at least three versions as veteran integration participant and research scholar; Judge Spurgeon Avakian, who, as Board of Education integration pioneer, gave me his interpretation of the political process of change; Jay Ball, whose doctoral thesis on environmental charge is drawn on in these pages; Ruth Barshay, who patiently read and edited; Iso Umeki and Phyllis Acton, who tirelessly typed and organized; Antonio Calabria, who documented references; Mabel Skrock, who praised me chapter by chapter as she typed; Robert Beyers, Director of News Services, Stanford University, who generously supplied us with school desegregation news; and last but far from least, Lou Ann Brower of Indiana University Press, who did a masterful job as editor.

I am sure there are many others. I thank them, one and all.

CONTENTS

FOREWORD

BEFORE I SAW NEIL SULLIVAN'S BOOK, I was indeed discouraged about school integration. My dream that one day in this country little black boys and girls and little white boys and girls would learn side by side in school had grown dim, as had many of my dreams of racial equality. At the rate school integration is progressing in the South, I figured that it will take 97 more years to bring it to accomplishment. I saw little more progress in the North where, although there is slightly more will and effort being applied to the problem, the task grows greater as the ghettos expand in impoverished, fenced-in numbers.

Then in May, 1967, I came to Berkeley to speak on the University of California campus and saw my friend, Dr. Sullivan. I heard his words and read in his book how, by a peaceful struggle through "the process of community change" as he calls it, total school integration in Berkeley, California, will hopefully be brought about by September, 1968. Hope returned to my soul and spirit.

I said as I addressed those 5,000 students, "There are times when you take a stand which is not safe nor politic nor popular. You take it because it is right." I was speaking of my opposition to the war in Viet Nam. Neil Sullivan, who also speaks out against our involvement in Viet Nam, is talking in this book about our deeper, our righteous, our non-violent struggle for democracy at home. His stand, like that to which I am now giving my energy, is not safe, nor politic nor popular. Only a few school superintendents the country over have the stamina and the skill to undertake the massive struggle for meaningful and full school integration.

But this Berkeley superintendent must win. He took his stand first in Prince Edward County, Virginia, where, against tremendous odds, he opened the Free Schools for Negro children deprived of education for three years because the county refused to integrate. He took his stand again in Berkeley where, just as he came in 1964, a strong drive to recall board members who had taken the first step in school integration was in progress. Three and one-half years later he was able to say, "The Board of Education has committed itself to total integration no later than September, 1968, and we shall make history on that day."

I am proud to know that it is my fellow Negroes who have pressed hardest for this victory supported by committed white parents. I am proud to know that they are willing to take on the greater burden.

"Now is the time" they told Superintendent Sullivan and he knew it well. I am honored that Dr. Sullivan has thus entitled his book. I repeat again and again what I said on that day of hope at the March on Washington, August 23, 1963, "Now is the time. Now is the time to make real the promise of democracy."

That promise has not been realized. We do not wait for its fulfillment; we work for it night and day. I believe that our schools must and can take the lead in this mighty effort. I believe that leaders like Dr. Sullivan can point the way.

MARTIN LUTHER KING, JR.

September 1967

Introduction

IT IS WITH DEEP FEELING that I name this book from the words of Martin Luther King, Jr. His urgent plea "Now is the time! Now is the time to make real the promise of democracy" has strengthened me as I have sought to fulfill that promise in the public schools. At times of discouragement I get out my record of the March on Washington in 1963, listen again to his ringing speech of hope, and am heartened to continue the struggle.

I first met him in 1962. He was speaking in Great Neck, Long Island, and I drove over to hear him from Old Westbury-East Williston, Long Island, where I was Superintendent of the school district. This evening marked the beginning of a series of events that impelled me to join the active fight for school integration. After he spoke, I asked his advice about bringing some Negro children up to our schools from Prince Edward County, Virginia—children who had not been in school for three years due to the county's refusal to integrate. Our schools had been sending clothing to Prince Edward, and textbooks for the use of northern teachers who flew down during weekends and vacations to give the children intervals of schooling.

Through Dr. King I later met Robert Kennedy, who, as United States Attorney General, had been ordered by President Kennedy to find some way to reopen the schools for Prince Edward County's Negro children, and was in the process of doing so. Robert Kennedy was always a major moral and financial supporter of Dr. King's Southern Christian Leadership Conference.

The following spring, in 1963, I went to Boston to be interviewed for the school superintendency; I had been recommended by my alma mater, Harvard University. Much as I liked my role in Long Island, this was my first big-time opportunity. But after a dinner meeting headed by Mrs. Louise Hicks, then Boston Board of Education President, I was bitterly disillusioned. Dr. King had led me into the battle against racial discrimination, and Boston, at that time, was no place to carry it forward. I fled back to Long Island where at least there was concern for the Prince Edward children.

I had barely entered my home when the telephone rang. A member of Robert Kennedy's staff was calling for the President of the United States, whom I had known for some time. Would I come to head the Free Schools Association that President Kennedy had just succeeded in organizing for the Negro children? I replied that I would think about it and let him know. But I knew right off what my answer would be. (I learned later that I was the only candidate.)

I must say that when a Kennedy asked me to take a job I was inclined to accept. I was one of the millions moved by President Kennedy's potent thrust. I was proud of his brilliance and courage, proud of him also as a Catholic who refused to be pressured by Catholic bureaucratic power. As an Irish-American, I shared a common heritage with him. The wealth and power of New England's lace curtain Irish was not a part of my background, however. My Irish grandmother had brought her brood to New England at the time of the Irish potato famine. My mother carried on with the Irish spirit. She saw education as the way out of the ghetto and Harvard as a distant dream.

I am often asked, "How did you get that way about integration?" My first motivation was my own experience in the Irish ghetto of Manchester, New Hampshire. My life there was not totally analogous to the experience of my Negro brothers, of course. I am white and invisible; I could fight my way up and out. But I know well the prejudice and discrimination and poverty that plague the black child.

My grandmother followed many other Irish families to the Irish ghetto in Manchester, New Hampshire, a mill town. My father, one of her nine children, had only two years of formal schooling and went to work for an uncle in a saloon at the age of eight, sweeping the floors and cleaning the spitoons. His brothers and sisters worked with other Irish youth 72 hours a week in the textile mills. My father advanced to beer runner, carrying buckets of beer to the textile workers' homes, and by 1918 he had advanced to head bartender in Manchester's leading hotel. Then came the Volstead Act enforcing prohibition, and he lost his job. He had many friends and, like most Irishmen, could have joined the police force or the fire department. But he was too proud to be eased, as a political favor, into that herd. Instead he took low-paying work in a local cigar factory.

My early childhood was spent in dingy, crowded tenements. We slept—three kids—in a cubicle without windows. Most of the windows we did have looked out on soot-covered walls. In winter we were often cold; in summer, uncomfortably hot. My mother was aggressive for her children. She knew one thing above all: schooling was of first importance, and the undermanned and overcrowded schools of the Irish ghetto were not good enough. Somehow she scraped together enough money to move the family to a very small home at the bottom of the hill on the edge of a middle- and upper-class neighborhood. For me,

Cornelius, five, the baby of the family, she forged a birth certificate to read that my legal age was six.

Down in the ghetto—our house was on its upper fringe —violence was a part of my everyday life. I fought and argued and cussed. In the new school I spent most of my time seeking recognition, and I used timeworn tactics— many young Negroes today entering a Caucasian school for the first time resort to them—pushing and shoving and playing pranks. Then I made a further mistake that set me apart—I came out for Al Smith for President in that Republican, Protestant, anti-Irish midst.

Like many of the impoverished Negro children I came to know many years later in Berkeley, I learned to speak two languages—the Irish brogue and phrases of my parents and their relatives, and the language of my middle-class schoolmates. In order to continue to high school, I became a fruit and vegetable peddler. My brothers and I bought a small second-hand wagon and sold our products from door to door in the ghetto.

When it came time for college, I could afford only the cheapest institution—nearby Keene Normal School. I was class president and an honor student, but when I was graduated in a class of over 300 students I was the last to be employed. In those days Catholics were not welcome as teachers in the New Hampshire public school systems. The only job I could get then, in 1936, was to be the one teacher in a one-room school in a poverty-stricken mountain area where I taught 48 children in eight grades. There I worked with children who suffered more than I had from hunger and cold. I loved those children, and I loved teaching, as I do now when I take time to do it. I managed to send part of my monthly pay of seventy dollars home to the family.

Then World War II and after it the G.I. Bill, which enabled me to take a year at Harvard. After several principalships and superintendencies, and after winning my Master's degree at Columbia, I went back to Harvard for my doctorate. It was a proud day for me when I was handed my diploma in the Harvard Yard. Now I could walk in the front door. Now my voice would be heard. And I could speak with authority to the isolated rural children I had first taught, "Get out of the rural ghetto, get on the bus to town and the wider learning world."

That is part of the story of how I "got that way." Commitment comes in many ways. It is a matter of heart and mind and imagination, perhaps of simply being an American who believes in democracy and is willing to work for it. But often the human spirit, filled with sympathy for and even personal experience of the problems of other men, fails to work actively to solve the problems. A spark is needed. Prince Edward County, Virginia, gave me that spark. The spirit of the Negro children and parents there, the great potential of the children, many of whom made up three years' school work in one, some of whom entered college the next year, fired my own spirit.

In Prince Edward County I also grew to understand the depth of the problem in the South. And the Supreme Court decision that finally reopened the Prince Edward public schools gave me the firm platform for integration of the schools.

In the spring of 1964, as the Prince Edward case went to the Supreme Court and my one-year term as Free Schools Superintendent was ending, I pondered my next move. After Prince Edward, it would be cowardly to return to the comfort of Old Westbury. Where could I go to carry on the work begun? At this point in my quandary, Spurgeon Avakian, then a member of the Berkeley Board of Education, came to Prince Edward to discuss the Berkeley superintendency, and I visited Berkeley. I was offered the position and accepted. Here I have come to learn the complexity of the problem in the North—and I have seen one solution.

After years of alternately stirring up and covering up the need for school integration by the community, the Berkeley school board had molded a rather shaky consensus to desegregate its secondary schools. The Ramsey Plan, named for the teacher who suggested it, would integrate the city's two junior high schools for all the city's seventh and eighth graders. The ninth graders, who previously had attended the junior high schools, would go to West Campus, a separate school related to Berkeley High School, the city's only high school. The desegregation plan would go into effect in September, 1964, at the new and novel all-ninth-grade West Campus, and at Garfield Junior High School, a prestigious, almost totally white school. The other junior high school—Willard—which already was racially mixed because of the diversity of the residents in the area, would enter the plan in 1966 when West Campus would be expanded.

The school board's feat of gaining approval for the Ramsey Plan was precarious. The plan was good, but consensus had been hard to win from the Garfield parents. Rumors of a board recall were growing. And the fate of elementary desegregation, which is infinitely more important, depended on the success of this one plan for integration of secondary education. I learned that the staff-recommended plan for elementary desegregation had been tabled "indefinitely" that same spring. Busing, an integral element in desegregation, was not to be considered. In sum, I could move cautiously, if at all, toward changing the composition of the elementary schools only after I had made the Ramsey Plan work.

A fighting chance, I concluded.

Four years later, in September, 1968, Berkeley became

the first United States city of over 100,000 with an almost even proportion of minority (41 per cent Negro) and Caucasian students, to totally desegregate its schools. I shall describe our lonely struggle in California, a state uncommitted to school integration in a nation where school integration, with a few exceptions, is not a reality. Berkeley's is a do-it-yourself community accomplishment. We offer it as a model for other communities which have the spirit and the fortitude to press ahead toward the day when "children will not be judged by the color of their skin but by the quality of their character."

1

Integration—Has Time Run Out?

I WRITE THIS FROM BERKELEY, CALIFORNIA, where black children and white children are riding buses up and down the hills to integrated schools. I want to inject hope into the present discouraging state of school integration. I believe that all children are born equal and should go to school together. I continue to believe that this seemingly simple concept will become part of the American way in spite of this country's white racism and increasing black separatism. I believe in school integration because I have seen it accomplished in this not untypical city.

What is happening in Berkeley could happen, I am sure, in any middle-sized city in the nation. But at this point it is not coming out that way.

The great majority of American children attend schools that are largely segregated. . . . Among minority groups, Negroes are by far the most segregated. Taking all groups, however, white children are most segregated. Almost 80 percent of all white pupils in first grade and twelfth grade attend schools that are from 90 to 100 percent white.

For Negro pupils, segregation is more nearly complete in the South . . . but it is extensive also in all the other regions where the Negro population is concentrated: the urban North, Midwest, and West. . . .

In its desegregation decision of 1954, the Supreme Court held that separate schools for Negro and white children are inherently unequal. This survey finds that, when measured by that yardstick, American public education remains largely unequal in most regions of the country, including all those where Negroes form any significant proportion of the population.*

To be specific, Berkeley is the only city of over 100,000 with a significant proportion (41 per cent) of Negro students to have totally desegregated its schools. A few smaller cities have desegregated, and a few cities have made some headway. Secondary school desegregation has been accomplished in a number of cities. Desegregation often begins in the secondary schools where the sensitive issue of busing young children does not have to be raised. Unfortunately the results are less significant at this level because meaningful integration—not merely desegregation—at ages 12 to 16 is difficult to achieve. It is almost too late for young people who have known only students of their own race during their first six or seven years of school.

Various communities have been struggling to find ways to achieve greater racial balance of elementary schools while retaining the neighborhood school. Busing, pairing,** redistricting, consolidating, and many other strategies have been tried. Many have failed; some have achieved at least partial success. I can list ten cities that have made progress. These are cities I helped study as a member of the United States Civil Rights Commission's Race and Education Advisory Committee. Our report which was given to the President in 1967, cited Berkeley and Riverside, California; Teaneck, Englewood, East Orange, and

*James S. Coleman, Johns Hopkins University. "Equality of Educational Opportunity." A publication of the National Center for Educational Statistics. U. S. Government Printing Office, Washington, 1966. Summary Report, p. 3.

**Pairing of two or more grades in adjacent attendance areas to achieve racial balance is the basis of the Princeton Plan, which Berkeley's present attendance zone plan follows.

Morristown, New Jersey; Rochester, Syracuse, and White Plains, New York; Hartford, Connecticut; Evanston, Illinois.

Berkeley has tried none of the patterns compatible with the neighborhood school concept. Our neighborhood schools—all-white hills, all-black ghetto—have changed into interracial schools. We bus the black children up to the hill schools for grades kindergarten through three. The white children ride down to the formerly black schools for fourth to sixth grades. The secondary schools were desegregated four years earlier.

Berkeley and the other examples present the hopeful part of the scene—a pitifully small part. The rest of the story is this: the "deliberate speed" in desegregation, ordered by the Supreme Court in 1954, did not follow. During the ensuing decade, the vast majority of black people and their leaders pleaded with the establishment to move to obey the Court's mandate. The Negroes were willing to do whatever was asked of them in order to have their children attend desegregated schools. They were willing to give up their own neighborhood schools, to see them closed and rejected as not good enough to house white children. They were willing to take the bus ride, to face danger as they went into the school gates, and to endure isolation within the classroom.

But what happened when the 1964 Civil Rights Law was finally enacted and enforcement was attempted? In the South, school boundaries were gerrymandered, hundreds of private schools for white children were established, Negro children were mobbed and terrorized as they enrolled, and many sat alone in the classrooms. As parents were threatened with loss of jobs, or lost them, as parents feared for their children's safety, many Negro children went back to their old schools and gave up the struggle. In one northern city after another, boards of education procrastinated, stalled, lied, vacillated, and maneuvered. They bought peace in their time by spending millions on surveys and studies, but never voted to take positive action. If action was taken, it was tokenism only—voluntary busing, futile and geared to fail; enforced busing of a couple hundred Negro children when there were many thousands, and even this threatened by massive parent boycotts.

Now, 14 years after the Supreme Court decision, I hear some of my black friends from Boston to San Francisco saying, "To hell with integration," "To hell with the Establishment," and "Burn, baby, burn!"

In 1967 the United States Commissioner of Education Harold Howe II was declaring in speeches all over the country that "the Nation's schools are almost as segregated today as they were in 1954." Token desegregation has been the rule in the South, and even this is "vastly countered" by circumvention of the law and the burgeoning of private schools for white children. In the cities of the North, school segregation "has grown massively" at the same time that more and more Negroes migrate into new and greater ghettos. That situation had certainly not changed in 1968; in fact, it has grown worse as our nation's efforts are concentrated on the Viet Nam war.

Our study* for the United States Civil Rights Commission reflects the disillusioning situation. We studied the few cities that were making progress. We also studied 19 cities cited as making no progress, or in fact, retrogressing.

> *Racial isolation in the public schools is intense throughout the United States. . . . In the Nation's metropolitan areas, where two-thirds of both the Negro and white population live, it is most severe. Seventy-five percent of the Negro*

---

*"Racial Isolation in the Public Schools," U. S. Commission on Civil Rights, 1967, Vol. 2, Appendix A, "Extent and Growth of Racial Isolation," pp. 2-7.

elementary students in the Nation's cities are in schools with enrollments that are nearly all-Negro. . . . while eighty-three percent of the white students are in nearly all-white schools. *Nearly nine of every ten Negro elementary students in the cities attend majority-Negro schools. . . .*

This high level of racial separation in city schools exists whether the city is large or small, whether the proportion of Negro enrollment is large or small, and whether the city is located North or South. . . .

Racial isolation in the public schools has been increasing. . . . There is evidence to suggest that once a school becomes almost half—or majority-Negro, it tends rapidly to become nearly all-Negro. . . .

In Southern and border cities, although the proportion of Negroes in all-Negro schools has decreased since the 1954 Supreme Court decision. . . . a rising Negro enrollment, with only slight desegregation, has produced a substantial increase in the number of Negroes attending nearly all-Negro schools. . . .

The Nation's metropolitan area populations are growing and are becoming increasingly separated by race. [Italics mine.]

Our "hot summers" began and grew longer. In the summer of 1966 teenage school dropouts exploded in Watts. The summer of 1967 brought bloody destruction in Newark, New Jersey, holocaust in Detroit, and rioting and burning in 50 other cities. In almost every case, the racial flareups were sparked by the young dropouts whom the ghetto schools had failed.

In the winter of 1967, John Gardner, United States Secretary of Health, Education and Welfare, said in an address to the American Statistical Association:

I believe we are now in a situation in which the gravest consequences for this nation will ensue if we fail to act decisively on the problems of the cities, poverty, and discrimination. . . . We are in deep trouble as a people. And history is not going to deal kindly with a rich nation that will not tax itself to cure its miseries.*

The following February (1968) Gardner resigned in despair and frustration when his programs were cut—Head Start, National Youth Corps, and others—because this country apparently was not "rich enough" to heal the problems of our cities and carry on the Viet Nam war at the same time, although President Johnson had at one time assured us of our capacity to do both. Our country was not even rich enough to provide free milk for hungry school children!

On March 3, 1968, the report of the National Advisory Commission on Civil Disorders, named to investigate the riots of summer, 1967, said, "If the Negro population as a whole developed even stronger feelings of being wrongly 'penned in' and discriminated against, many of its members might come to support not only riots, but the rebellion now being preached by only a handful" (p. 397).

City by city, the commission explored the history of Negro grievances. In Atlanta, Georgia, a city which has moved forward impressively in integration, the commission found that "the economic and educational gap between the black and white populations may, in fact, have been increased." In Detroit, a city cited by sociologists as having made more progress toward solving interracial problems than any other city, the commission reported that "in the inner city schools, more than half the pupils who entered high school became dropouts."

What have we done to these young people? It is really what we have *not* done. In the South, denial of school integration by persecution, deviation, and establishment of private schools for whites. Across the North, futile and

*Saturday Review, March 16, 1968. Quoted in an editorial by James Cass.

minimal efforts, frustrated by masses of anti-busing parents.

Has time run out? Is it possible for any community to integrate its schools while George Wallace and Lester Maddox and many like them spout racism and white power and Rap Brown and Stokeley Carmichael advocate the use of guns and threaten to "burn out" and "shut out" Whitey? Is it possible for one middle-sized city with the familiar array of white bigots capable of flooding the mails with hate literature, one city surrounded by cities full of racism—both white and black—to succeed?

The answer in this city of Berkeley is a resounding "YES." "Yes," from a large majority of the black community. A quiet "Yes" from the Orientals who have long supported our schools' forward moves. A sturdy "Yes" from the teachers and their organizations, without whose support the difficult task could not have been begun. And the loudest "Yes" from the children themselves, the uncontaminated young—white and black—who have not yet been infected by the virus of racism.

As I write this book little black children are mounting the bus to the white hill schools and white children are riding the bus to the schools of the ghetto.

2

Integration—Why?

THE RATIONALE FOR SCHOOL INTEGRATION IS VERY SIMPLE. It is also very old and very obvious. "Because it is the law," we say. And "Because it is right."

Because it is the law? Why did we need a law? Every man's rights, the black man's and the white man's, are inherent in nature, and our Declaration of Independence proclaims: "We hold these truths to be self-evident: that all men are created equal; that they are endowed by their Creator with certain inalienable rights. . . ." Yet the Negro's rights have not been respected from the beginning of our nation. Originally each Negro counted as only three-fifths of a man when determining political representation. One human being, three-fifths of his democratic rights. After the Civil War this gross injustice was rectified, at least on the official document, the Constitution. But it seemed that the freed slave could not be a free citizen. We needed laws to guarantee the black man freedom to practice his human rights. Two hundred years after the birth of this nation the first such law was enacted.

Now that civil rights laws are on the books Americans have been devising ways to get around them. Americans have a poor record on obeying laws that interfere with their personal way of life.

How about the "because it's right" answer? This high moral stance rings hollowly in the face of our history.

Morality has not prevailed and does not prevail in this professedly Christian country. Nor has it been our primary motivation. As Commager points out in *The American Mind,** we have always had an obsession with moralizing, and thus rationalizing all our actions. We speak in moral terms but act in radically different ways. Where does the Golden Rule come in for the white man who moves out of the block when a Negro moves in, or who moves out of the school district when Negroes move into the school, or to the realtor who makes money by expediting the process?

Morality? In the name of morality, white Americans "have been good" to their black cooks and maids while ignoring the living conditions of their families, have contributed to the NAACP and the United Crusade while fleeing from incoming black neighbors and/or integrated schools. "Our white Americans have had a genius for separating their idealism and their practice," says the report of the President's Commission on Civil Disorders.

Too many Americans have tried to hide from the real problems when they say, "I am for integration because it is right." "But," they always add. "But let's wait until *they* (the Negroes) are ready," or "until they've come *up* to our educational level," or "until our socio-economic and educational levels are in balance." Some even say, "until they've *earned* it." I have taken these quotes from The Open Forum Column in Berkeley's local paper, the *Berkeley Daily Gazette.* The attitude is one of superiority, of charity "handed down," of "giving" the Negroes equality. No, the conscientious "because it is right" approach is not enough to bring about integration.

The "why" I emphasize is this: because both the black child and the white child need integration. Integrated schools can get the black child, psychologically at least,

*Henry Steele Commager, *The American Mind,* Yale University Press, 1950.

out of the ghetto. In educational terms, the integrated school can raise his achievement level, can give him a stronger self-image and a sense of control of his destiny. Let me cite Coleman's *Equality of Educational Opportunity*,* a distinguished volume of research:

> Those pupils who first entered integrated schools in the early grades record consistently higher scores than the other groups. . . . For children from disadvantaged groups, achievement or lack of achievement appears closely related to what they believe about their environment: whether they believe the environment will respond to reasonable efforts, or whether they believe it is instead merely random or immoveable. . . . It may well be, then, that *one of the keys toward success for minorities which have experienced disadvantage and a particularly unresponsive environment— either in the home or the larger society—is a change in this conception. . . .*
>
> An education in integrated schools can be expected to have major effects on attitudes toward members of other racial groups. At its best, it can develop attitudes appropriate to the integrated society these students will live in; at its worst, it can create hostile camps of Negroes and whites in the same school. Thus, there is more to "school integration" than merely putting Negroes and whites in the same building, and there may be more important consequences of integration than its effect on achievement.

School integration can change attitudes—that is the key factor in my estimation. It can erase fear and prejudice. It can erase discrimination by the major society. It can erase racism. It can change hearts, minds, and the kind of action for which this nation stands indicted. It can enable the black child to take an equal part in the world, to have the kind of job he wants, the kind of house he wants, the kind of life he wants. The black child, educated in an

*James S. Coleman, *Equality of Educational Opportunity,* a publication of the National Center for Educational Statistics, U. S. Government Printing Office, Washington, 1966. p. 321

integrated school from his early years, can emerge from his "ghetto-ized" concept. He can become a partner of his white fellows. He will not be a second-class citizen if he neither thinks nor feels like one. The white child in turn can grow up with his black school companions—in the classroom, on the playground, at camp—uncontaminated by the prejudice that has infected his elders. It is our hope that in the integrated school we shall not raise another generation of bigots.

As I write this, I think of my Black Power friends— both my contemporaries and the many black students I listen to. I think of the rising surge of Black Power in Berkeley, greater in Oakland to the south and San Francisco across the Bay, and widespread across the nation as the demands for separatism grow. I understand the exhilaration and hope that is felt, especially by the young, in the concept Black Power. "Black"—a word now used with pride—reminding the black American of his uniqueness and importance through Afro-American history. Indeed "Black is beautiful." And "Power"—power to be free, equal *and* unique. Power through education, identity, awareness of black history and black culture. Power through common bonds of black consciousness and mutual standards of beauty, conduct, and accomplishment. Black Power.

Black Power to do what? I believe there must be black student power, black teacher power, black citizen power— decision-making power. The Black Student Union at Berkeley High School understands this. When racial trouble exploded at Berkeley's Garfield Junior High School following the assassination of Martin Luther King, Jr., it was the Black Student Union leaders who cooled it down. They spoke to their angry brothers:

> We consider ourselves big brothers to black students at Garfield, Willard, and West Campus. We want to help you get organized so you can "meet the man." [Eddie Creamer, president]

White America's problem is us. And once you realize this, you know that gaining our freedom depends upon our being intelligent. The only way to do that is to hit the books, learn what the white man knows so that you can compete with him and get on top. Those of you who run around beating heads in the name of Dr. Martin Luther King or black power don't know what you're talking about. Black power is brain power. (Earl McCann, vice-president)

That's it—brain power. And the place to get it is the integrated school. Shared power, I'd call it. Power, 50-50. If, however, Black Power becomes black racism, I am against it. I would agree with Roy Wilkins, president of the NAACP, who said in an address at the University of California on March 23, 1968: "Black racism will only repeat the tragic monologue."

"We are the same but different." We want integrated schools *and* black power, many Negroes are saying. Dr. Robert Coles shared this insight of a Negro boy with us during the spring of 1968 when we were preparing for total integration in the Berkeley schools. Dr. Coles, a psychologist from Harvard University, spent part of that time with us. He too believed that Negroes are both the same and different, and after several years of studying Northern and Southern Negro children as they rode buses to integrated schools, he was able to say, "If we put our similarities and our differences together, we can make, even now, at this late date, a wonderful society."

That is the "why" of integration. If I, as an education leader, stand alone, I shall stand for integration.

3

Integration—By Law?

"THERE'S NO TRUTH IN THE OLD REFRAIN that you can't legislate civil rights," Supreme Court Justice Thurgood Marshall reminded us, at the University of California's Charter Day ceremonies on March 23, 1968. Yet today, 14 years after the Supreme Court mandate to desegregate, our schools are more segregated than before, and I would amend his statement by saying that legislation is not enough. Civil laws must be aggressively enforced.

Enforcement is particularly crucial to providing equal educational opportunities. Most judicial decisions on racial imbalance in the schools place the problem of how to correct it firmly in the laps of the executive and legislative branches of state and federal governments. The courts point out the inequity and order the appropriate governmental body to do something about it, sometimes but not always with a deadline. Only five states have enacted laws aimed at ending school segregation, only two have aggressively enforced the laws.

The federal Civil Rights Acts of 1957 and 1960 accomplished almost nothing in school desegregation. President Kennedy stirred the nation to action with his spirited "Let us begin." As the wave of grief over his death swept the nation, President Johnson carried on with "Let us continue." And he continued—until our Viet Nam involvement preoccupied his activities. Courageously he pushed

[1 3]

through the Civil Rights Act of 1964 which provides federal funds to encourage local school systems to desegregate. The funds are made available primarily for technical assistance, which covers consultation in developing guidelines for desegregation, estimating racial composition, studying organization alternatives, preparing teaching staff through in-service training, developing new curriculum materials suitable for racially mixed classrooms, and developing community participation. Other provisions of the law act in a negative way to stop segregation. Title VI of the Act says that funds will be withheld or cut off when districts fail to take steps adequate to eliminate dual (separate but equal) schools. It also authorizes the Attorney General to bring action in the name of the United States against districts which try to avoid desegregating by giving up federal aid. Thus Congress gave school districts "freedom of choice" to desegregate with or without federal funds.

What happened in the 11 Southern states at which the law was at first specifically aimed? Token integration began. Almost all districts submitted desegregation plans to the Government and received their federal aid. But soon even that minimal integration declined as Negro children and their parents succumbed to the persecution they encountered. Funds continued to be accepted, however, even though the recipients were not carrying out the law. If court action was initiated, the case stayed on the books of the bogged-down courts. Every circuitous way known to man was used to evade the law and keep the money.

Then, in 1966, Title VI was revised. New guidelines appeared to strengthen the law. For example, systems assigning pupils under freedom-of-choice plans must produce actual desegregation figures that meet standards set by the Government. There must be significant integration of teaching staffs. Small, inferior school units operated to "contain" racial minorities must be abandoned. And finally, school systems were required to report just how much faculty integration was anticipated.

But in April, 1967, the United States Office of Education released enrollment figures from the South showing a startling number of free-choice districts coming up with less desegregation than they had in 1966. Many Negro students were asking for transfer back to their old schools after harassment from white students, white teachers, and white parents. And many Negro parents were being threatened by loss of work, or were losing their jobs, if their children chose to try to attend desegregated schools. Also, transferring from their traditionally inferior schools, the Negro pupils were finding the new classes too difficult academically, and white teachers were doing little to help them adjust and learn. In the experience of federal compliance officers, local officials were not doing enough to make free-choice plans work.

Meanwhile, the ability of the Department of Health, Education and Welfare to enforce compliance was jeopardized by lack of funds. A body blow was struck when Congress cut the budget of Secretary of Health, Education and Welfare, John Gardner, to a minimal and totally inadequate amount.

Ever since the Civil Rights Act was passed in 1964, private schools for white children have burgeoned throughout the South. Existing private schools expanded, and new ones sprang up in church basements, abandoned stores— anywhere room was found. At the abortive White House Conference "To Fulfill These Rights" in May, 1966, Ben Brooks, a white school principal in the black belt of Enfield, North Carolina, told me that in his area alone, 33 new private schools had been opened. That same spring the founder of Prince Edward Academy in Farmville, Virginia, estimated that since 1959, 160 similar white schools had been established in the South. The growth has been most marked in communities where extensive integration has been ordered by federal authorities, and in many of these communities the private school organizers have succeeded in completely defeating the intent of integration orders.

Civil rights lawyers say that under current court rulings there is no way to stop segregationists from setting up private schools. When the big push for private schools began in 1964 predictions were made that such schools would not last because of limited funds and the educational inexperience of their founders. But they have survived and most have flourished, so far as attendance goes. Many white parents are so strongly opposed to integration that they will make tremendous financial sacrifice to pay private school tuition. Also many are willing to sacrifice the quality of their children's education, to send them to such makeshift quarters to be taught by ill-trained teachers, to preserve segregation.

It is true that a number of small school districts have quietly obeyed the letter of the law and permitted token desegregation to take place. It is true that Texas leads the Southern states with 34.6 per cent of its schools now desegregated. But in the South as a whole, only 6 per cent of the schools have desegregated. Meanwhile as machines take over the job of the field workers, Southern Negroes have migrated in great numbers to the North—into urban ghettos where the same old pattern of segregation prevails, where the law has been observed only in rare instances, and where evasion of the law has succeeded as generally as in the South.

Take Chicago, for one example. Former Superintendent of Schools Ben Willis (dubbed "Ben the Builder") took advantage of Federal funds made available to desegregate the schools under the 1964 Civil Rights Act and went on building one neighborhood school after another. When Francis Keppel, then United States Commissioner of Education, froze the funds on charges of deliberate segregation, Chicago politicians pressured Washington to free the funds again. And Keppel lost his job.

When Willis retired, he was replaced by James F. Redmond, who devised an imaginative plan featuring educational parks to desegregate the schools. Several grades from neighborhood schools would be grouped together on one campus under the concept of educational parks. The large school would then be broken down into several schools within a school in which specialized teaching, student aid, and independent work by an individual student could be encouraged. But in the spring of 1968, all Redmond had been able to accomplish was to bus 249 Negro pupils to white schools, and this in the face of white boycotts and near riots.

No, the great landmark Civil Rights Act of 1964 has not accomplished its purpose. It authorized the Attorney General to bring school desegregation suits in certain circumstances, empowered the Commissioner of Education to give technical and financial assistance to desegregated school districts, and gave the Department of Health, Education, and Welfare the power to withhold financial assistance from school districts that discriminated. But sanctions were not clearly imposed. Neither the courts nor state authorities generally required school districts to overcome racial imbalance. Ways to get around the law were found.

Consider the five states I have mentioned as the *only* states that took action to enforce the law. On August 18, 1965, shortly after the law was enacted, Massachusetts Governor John A. Volpe signed the nation's first state law to enforce racial balance in schools. A combination of financial penalties and incentives was intended to spur action. It was considered a model law. It gave the State

Commissioner of Education power to require school boards to create racial balance and, if they did not, to withhold state aid. But what happened in Massachusetts? Dr. Owen B. Kiernan, State Education Commissioner, fought hard to enforce the law. The most notable instance was in 1966 when he led a battle to force the Boston School Committee to take steps to comply. He lost the battle, as the school committee said he demanded too much and civil rights groups said he did not demand enough. In the spring of 1968 he resigned.

In New York state, on the other hand, Commissioner of Education James Allen has aggressively enforced its law modeled after that of Massachusetts. The first case he won was in Manhasset, Long Island, then one of the richest suburbs in the United States, where the Negroes were moved from their school into the white schools. Syracuse is moving toward an educational park as a means of desegregation. Rochester is pioneering in busing Negro pupils to suburban schools. Other cities are moving.

Michigan, again with a state law modeled after that of Massachusetts, has changed from the system of electing a state superintendent at $15,000 a year to appointing one at $30,000. The new appointee is Ira Polley, a dynamic young man who appears to be ready and able to enforce the law.

In New Jersey the battle to integrate was won in Englewood in the early 1960's under the spirited leadership of State Superintendent Mark Shedd, now superintendent in Philadelphia. Progress in the large cities of New Jersey has been slow despite aggressive attempts to implement the law by State Commissioner Dr. Carl L. Marburger.

And now we come to California where we also have a law. A detailed racial survey of California's public school system in 1966—the first done in any American state— showed that in California cities, where most Negroes live,

85 per cent of Negro children attend minority schools. Dorman L. Commons, then State Board of Education president, called it "in many ways a frightening report." He said: "In spite of the fact that we have made what we thought were heroic efforts to break the ignorance cycle, there is very strong evidence that we are not making progress."

Five counties contain more than 78 per cent of the state's Negro pupils; they are Alameda (Berkeley is in Alameda County), Contra Costa, Los Angeles, San Diego, San Francisco. In the face of these facts, the State Board brought out the shocking action of county officials in various parts of California who had been advising local school boards that it is unnecessary or even illegal to set school attendance boundaries with the aim of improving racial balance. The board acted to "chastize" these county councils for justifying de facto segregation. And Dr. Max Rafferty, State Superintendent of Public Instruction, sent out a mild memo reviewing the law.

"State policies," he said, "explicitly state that school districts have a legal obligation to take reasonably affirmative steps to prevent the segregation of students in schools by race, regardless of the cause of segregation, and to consider the ethnic composition of a school in determining its attendance boundaries." He cited the California Supreme Court decision in 1963 in *Jackson v. Pasadena School District* which stated: "The right to an equal opportunity for education and the harmful consequences of segregation require that school boards take steps, insofar as reasonably feasible, to alleviate racial imbalance in schools regardless of its cause."

In 1968 the same state superintendent, who reminded us that "school districts have a legal obligation to take reasonably affirmative steps to prevent the segregation of students in schools by race," ran for the United States Senate as "California's Foremost Friend of Neighborhood Schools."

There is a movement in California to follow Michigan's lead in appointing rather than electing the State Superintendent. If Rafferty resigns, this movement may grow. But whom could we expect Governor Ronald Reagan to appoint? Whom could we expect the current State Board of Education to advise him to appoint? Governor Reagan has replaced most of the liberal-minded members of the board by political reactionaries.

No, at this time we cannot expect much, if any support for integration from the law and its authorized enforcers in California.

In the face of the state's impotence, I looked forward in March, 1968, to the Federal Title VI guidelines for northern cities. I had helped to write them. I had waited and waited for the final version to arrive on my desk. I read with approval the lengthy key sections on "Equal Educational Opportunity," "Inferior Educational Facilities and Services," and "School Planning, Construction, and Attendance Zones." These were the directions I had helped write; these were the guidelines that could move our cities before it is too late.

But then I went back to the introduction, seeking the escape clause, hoping that there was none. But here it was —the language that weakens the case for enforcement:

Student Assignment. School systems are responsible for the elimination of discrimination on the ground of race, color, or national origin in the assignment of students to schools, classes and activities. In particular, school systems may not establish or maintain school attendance zones, school feeder patterns, or school transportation patterns; great transfers from school to school or school system to school system; or assign students to curricula, classes, or activities at schools in a manner designed to segregate students on the basis of race, color, or national origin.

And then this: *"Although racial imbalance may indicate discriminatory school assignment, it does not of itself establish discrimination."* [Italics mine.]

As I read those words, I realized once again that de facto segregation is not going to be abolished through the Civil Rights Act. Committed superintendents will have to go it alone. Berkeley will have to go it alone. It must be a do-it-yourself process.

4

Berkeley As A Target
For Integration

BERKELEY, A CITY OF 121,300, holds within it all the forces that are shaping every interracial city in this country. The problems of the city are typical; the difference is that, during recent years at least, its citizens have recognized and faced up to these problems. Since 1964 I came to know the city well. I loved it from the first and my devotion grows. My life encompassed every area of the city—the hill where I lived, the District Administration Building in north Berkeley where I worked, the schools and homes I visited up and down and across the city, the City Hall where I consulted with the Mayor as a member of The Future of Berkeley Committee, the YMCA where I swam, the Bay where I sailed, the bridges I crossed, and of course, the University.

Berkeley, one of the most beautiful cities in the nation and the world, is flavored by the intellectual and political life of the University of California with its 27,500 students, outstanding faculty, and 24-acre campus extending from the business district to the hills. The Negro community, which is taking an increasing role in the city's political and educational growth, contributes its own diverse and essential ingredients to the mix. And the city is peppered by a persistent group of embittered reactionaries.

In sum, Berkeley is progressive, permissive, aesthetic, sophisticated, liberal, activist, and far out. It also has its conservative, reactionary, and racist elements.

Berkeley's 121,300 citizens, compactly enclosed between the eastern hills and San Francisco Bay, embraces many minority groups. By far the largest minority is Negro —more than one-third of the general population and 41 per cent of the approximately 17,000 school population. By and large, the rich and upper middle-class residents live high in the hills, the poor (mostly Negro) in the flats where housing merges with light industry that skirts the Bay, and the middle and some lower middle-class residents in middle Berkeley. Nine per cent of Berkeley's residents are in the upper class according to a socio-economic scale, 20 per cent upper middle, 26 per cent middle, and 25 per cent lower middle, and 20 per cent just plain poor.

The poor live in an area which is not a sprawl, due to limited space, and which definitely is not a slum. Most of the homes of the poor are neatly painted, pleasantly gardened, and proudly kept. But the area where the Negro poor, as well as its upper border where the Negro middle class lives, *is* a ghetto, in the shut-in, shut-out meaning of the term. By a small majority, Berkeley voted against a local fair housing ordinance in 1962. The rationale was that the state fair housing law was sufficient if it were more strongly enforced. In 1964 Berkeley was one of the few northern California cities to vote to maintain the state fair housing law during a referendum; a large majority of Berkeley defended the law. However most Californians voted to nullify the law for several years and a weakened form of the law is now on the books. Fair housing does not prevail in this atmosphere of ambivalence; the University student renters are the one exception. Students are housed interracially in the dormitories and cooperatives, and discrimination against those who rent off-campus housing is not allowed, as landlords are well aware. Berkeley has its enclaves of low-income, small-home owners who, feeling threatened and insecure, resist both housing and school integration. Neither they, nor the affluent residents of the hills, have permitted more than a handful of Negroes to buy homes in their midst. There are only a very few realtors in Berkeley who will try to find a house in a white block for a Negro client.

Nor does fair employment prevail, in spite of the efforts of most business and industrial establishments as well as the University to hire more persons from minority groups. Among Negroes the unemployment rate is about 20 per cent, as compared with the total city unemployment rate of 4 per cent. Among the young Negroes, aged 16 to 24, the unemployment rate is 28 per cent.

The University, which employs approximately one-third of the city's 50,000 gainfully employed, has a comparatively good record. About one-fifth of its employees holding nonacademic jobs are from minority and the largest number of these are Negro. And it is vigorously recruiting more. However, only 25 members of the faculty are from minority groups. And in its student body, only 500 belong to minority groups. Here again major efforts are being made to recruit, to tutor minority youth in special programs to bring them up to admission standards, to bend requirements, to give help where needed among those who enroll. In April, 1968, the Ford Foundation granted $500,000 to the University's School of Social Work to bring in minority trainees. There is a striking lack of Negroes in the School of Education. Only twenty-five black students graduated from the University of California with teaching credentials in the 1965-66 school year; just four Mexican-Americans graduated as trained teachers that year.

Berkeley is exceptional in the fact that there has been no mass exodus of whites as the Negro population gained in proportion. When we desegregated our secondary schools in 1964, vociferous threats to move from Berkeley were raised, but in fact, few families are willing to pick up and leave this city. Berkeley has no suburbs and this may have been a factor in keeping whites here, but there are plenty of all-white suburban-type communities to the north and south, and over the hill in Contra Costa county where dissatisfied Berkeleyans could have gone.

Our school censuses have shown that the Caucasian-Negro balance has stabilized during the interval when secondary school desegregation had been accomplished and elementary integration was in the planning stage. Specifically, the 1966 census found a gain of 132 Caucasian students and the 1967 census showed a gain of 24, as contrasted to the former pattern of a yearly loss of 300. During the same period the yearly increase in Negro students declined from 1.5 to 2 per cent to .5 per cent. This relative stability in racial proportion, held over three consecutive annual censuses—and in a period of change and integration—gives us great hope that we are successfully maintaining a racially balanced school community.*

If people did begin to move out of Berkeley, there would be one reasonable explanation. The cost of living is extremely high. Housing is at least 10 per cent higher than in most cities. Food—even California fruit and vegetables —comes at peak prices. While average effective buying power is high—$2,870 per capita and $7,933 per household —a breakdown shows that almost one-third of the buyers are in the lowest income bracket. Thirty-two per cent are in the 0-$2,999 income bracket, 14 per cent in the $3,000-$4,999, 25.6 per cent in the $5,000-$7,999, 9.4 per cent in the $8,000-$9,999 and 17.5 per cent in the $10,000 a year and over. And total tax rate in Berkeley reached a high of $13.80 in 1968.

But people come, people stay, and those who move sell

*I must explain that the student racial census, taken by the Berkeley district occasionally since 1960 and required by the state since 1966, is a "visual" census only, made by visual observation of each classroom by the teacher. No student is asked his race.

their homes at a large profit. There are many reasons why they come and why they stay—the equable climate, of course; the city's beauty; the cultural richness; the permissive atmosphere; the general excitement and ferment which, because no winter snows and ice chill the process, goes on all year-round.

Berkeley has one of the first council-city manager systems of government to be developed in California. During recent years the city council has been dominated by strong liberals and at present almost all of its nine members, including Mayor Wallace Johnson, could be classed as liberals—philosophically and politically. A few are moderate Republicans, most are Democrats, one could be called New Left. Two members are Negroes. Mayor Johnson won distinction for by his sturdy, brilliant, and victorious fight to put the Bay Area Rapid Transit system (currently being built) underground instead of partially overhead, as first scheduled. The Mayor, inventor and manufacturer of aluminum escalated structures, erected one of his own towers in the area just south of middle Berkeley to dramatize the effect of "another wall" between the city's hills and flatlands residents.

Ever since I came to Berkeley, and long before, I'm told, the two hot issues before the city council have been dog-leashing and urban cleanliness and beauty. Dogs, from prize-winners to mongrels, are much loved and compose a high proportion of the city's population. Dogs are everywhere, and so are the beautiful gardens and walks that many dogs desecrate and damage. On May 13, 1968, Mike Culbert wrote in the *Berkeley Daily Gazette,* "a tidal wave of demands for a dog leash ordinance have rained forth on City Hall;" he had disdain for Berkeley's "continual fetish on beauty." Yet, in spite of periodical outbursts by the beauty-lovers and the endless hours spent in argument before the council, no dog leash law had been passed at the time of writing.

The same permissiveness extends to the city's hippies, who, in part, have been responsible for the Berkeley image and the Berkeley type. Berkeley was one of the first and favorite hippie centers. The Block on Telegraph Avenue, which runs into the University campus, was their gathering place. Here the flower girls and the boys, teenage to 30, stroll the street, their long hair flying, in the dress of the American Indian, the Civil War soldier, the covered wagon pioneer, the Hindu mystic, or whatever they can find in attics or Army Surplus stores. Some sit in front of book stores or art shops meditating, some playing flutes. Some sell underground papers or *The Barb,* a politically radical, shocking, top-selling weekly owned and edited by a one-time follower of H. L. Mencken. Some man the interesting book and poster shops. Children and dogs run free, flowers and beads and bells are everywhere.

The Block is, of course, a police problem—its main hazards presented by those who turn on with LSD or other chemicals, runaways, and teenagers' attraction to the scene. The problem climaxed in several events when the hippies closed off the Block. To "contain" the hippies, Berkeley's police chief persuaded the city council to sponsor a "Family Happening for Peace in Berkeley" every Sunday in Civic Center Park. These Sunday happenings, complete with folk-rock bands, balloons, free soft drinks and ice cream cones, draw a happy crowd of hippies with their kids and dogs, as well as a number of interested "straights."

"The Berkeley image" and "the Berkeley type" have been drawn also from the University's student activists. For years the University of California at Berkeley has been the vanguard of social action and revolt. In 1954 it was the setting of the faculty fight against the state loyalty oath, in 1964, the student Freedom of Speech movement. Since 1966 campus groups have led local and sometimes national opposition to the Viet Nam war and the draft, have waged a continual struggle for more voice in university policy, and have spoken out for civil rights.

Although only a minority of the students share the hippie life, the Block is so close to the campus plaza where the activists hold forth that observers automatically lump the two together as the Berkeley type. University Chancellor Roger Heyns has plenty of trouble correcting the public's image of the typical Berkeley student. When he travelled around the state during the University demonstrations he used a good story from his personal life, one familiar to many parents. He came upon his son in his room in such a sprawl of clothes, sports equipment, books, and guitars that there was scarcely room to stand or sit. "Why don't you clean up this mess?" His son looked amazed. "What mess?" he asked.

What mess, indeed. The mess in Berkeley is in the main a great force for a better world. The under-30 crowd who are protesting and demonstrating are witnessing with their lives for their beliefs.

Too often critics fail to include in the general category of Berkeley activists those who join the Peace Corps—four times as many at U. C. as the national rate per thousand—and the more than 2,000 students who volunteer as tutors in the ghettos, prisons, and schools of the Bay Area. And hundreds of them tutor in the Berkeley schools through the School Resource Volunteers.

It is said that *everything* happens in Berkeley. This is true—and it usually happens here first and the most. When Martin Luther King addressed a student crowd on the campus in May of 1967, he declared: "Berkeley has stirred the conscience of the academic world and of America."

Along with its students, Berkeley's hills and flats and middle ground are full of scholars, social pioneers, artists, and writers. The University has the highest number of Nobel Prize winners of any faculty in the United States.

The Berkeleyans who care deeply for the natural and human resources cut across University and town lines. The Save the Bay crusade, which is resulting in state legislation to prevent filling parts of San Francisco Bay for land development, started here. The Save the Redwoods movement to maintain Northern California's primeval forests from the lumber industry is strongly active here; a Berkeleyan has been the long-time pioneer and leader of the Save the Redwoods League.

Berkeley was the home of the late Alexander Meiklejohn, great scholar and worker for civil rights, and the Meiklejohn Library, named for him, is the main—if not only—source for lawyers fighting civil rights cases in the South.

Berkeley is the home of Byron Rumford, first Negro to be elected to the California State Assembly, a fearless battler for civil rights and author of the state's Fair Housing Act.

Berkeley has ten per cent of the brightest public school students in the United States. Berkeley High School Negro students have been among the first of their race to win national scholarship awards.

Berkeley has more volunteers per square foot than any city I ever lived in. School Resource Volunteers number 500 adults and college students who type, tutor, and work with children in art, music, and drama. SRV also has a community pool of business and professional men and University professors who add their talents as speakers, artists, and performers to the educational program.

Berkeley is also replete with "Old Blues," University graduates who have lived on in the city, glorifying the good old days. Some of them join in the vilification of today's activists and whatever criticism of the public schools that is going on. "They're not the way they were when I went to school," is their rationale. As the flacks propagandize for people to come to California "where life is better," and as an estimated 1,000 a day pour in, their slogan is "Keep California for Californians."

Berkeley's one newspaper, the *Daily Gazette,* harks back to earlier, simpler days. When I came in September, 1964, the paper was vigorously supporting the recall of the school board members who favored desegregation of the secondary schools.

Berkeley is the chosen residence of many retired people, some of whom are inclined to vote against the schools because their children, if any, are long since grown. Our city is the favorite setting for "Little Old Lady" stories— usually "little old ladies in tennis shoes." Berkeley's little old ladies come in two styles, however. One version—a sturdy intellectual whose tennis shoes are probably English-made—can be found attending civil rights meetings and demonstrations, and marching staunchly in those shoes. She votes for us. The other version is the well-heeled old lady who dons expensive clothes and a flowered hat for lunch at some posh private club. She does not vote for us.

Berkeley is an overworked target of the State Burns Subcommittee on Un-American Activities, which has smeared the University's student activists, professors, and President with distorted and false charges of Communism, immorality, and subversion. Not content with endangering the University, this committee in 1966 also reached over into Berkeley's Garfield Junior High School, alleging "pro-Communist teaching." The charge was based on a question given for a homework assignment: "Why is it important for us to study Russia?" Two Berkeley intern teachers had their credentials threatened in the winter of 1966 because they had participated in the Sproul Hall Freedom of Speech Movement sit-in. The Board of Education, my administration, and both local teacher organizations joined in opposing the withholding of their credentials for having acted according to their consciences. Fortunately, after a hearing before the State Credentials Committee, the threat was removed and they received their credentials on schedule.

This is Berkeley. At once typical and far out. A thriving American city, a good place to live and work, and yet not self-satisfied. John Miller, a former president of the Berkeley School Board, said of the schools: "The problems of Berkeley's educational system are in fine the problems of America and the world. The difference here is that we recognize that fact." The same can be said of the Berkeley community.

5

Evolution of a Revolution

BERKELEY IS COOL IN SUMMER, as visitors soon find out when they pour in from the East in their seersucker suits and thin summer dresses. It is hot only for a few three-day intervals in late September or early October when all the pampered natives think they will die of the unaccustomed heat. And then the cool fog blows in.

The weather was cool when I came to Berkeley as the new Superintendent of Schools in September, 1964. But mood and tempers were climbing way up the thermometer. On the University of California campus the Freedom of Speech students were demonstrating; the massive sit-in was not far off. The cruel Proposition 14, a move launched by the realtors to knock out California's Fair Housing Act, aroused Berkeley's many liberals to join a "No on 14" drive to defeat it.

In my domain, the public schools, all hell had broken loose. An independent group, the Parents Association for Neighborhood Schools (PANS) was out to punish the Board of Education for approving the Ramsey Plan for desegregating secondary schools, and to prevent desegregation from going further. PANS—a mixture of a few intellectuals, upper- and middle-class conservatives, Berkeley Citizens United (its majority, Birch Society types), and lower middle-class homeowners—was waging a strong fight to recall the school board members responsible for

Berkeley's move toward ending de facto segregation. PANS called it a revolution.

It was a revolution. How had this revolution come about? How had the Berkeley school system developed from a very conservative, traditional status quo school board and school administration into one committed to progress and change? In doctoral thesis terms, it was "Organizational Adaptation to Environmental Pressures."* This study and the lively, outspoken report on "The Politics of Educational Change" in Berkeley given by Superior Court Judge Spurgeon Avakian, former school board member and integration pioneer, at a conference of University of California teacher internes,** tell much about the seeds of the revolution and its growth.

In 1939, the United States Census showed Berkeley's population as 93.8 per cent Caucasian, 4 per cent Negro. In 1947, 12.8 per cent of the city was Negro. Currently, Berkeley is approximately one-third Negro. From the 4 per cent in 1939 Negro school enrollment rose to 37 per cent in 1963. At this time, as I have said, it is 41 per cent.

In the old days Berkeley's small Negro population in the flats was quiet and "well-behaved." Berkeley's "old" Negro residents were characterized as conservative and happy with their treatment over the years and were looked upon by school administrators as a "good" group of stable people who would not cause a fuss. As Dr. Ball reports in his thesis, a committee of Negro residents was appointed to greet newcoming Negroes and tell them how a good Negro

*Jay Tracy Ball, *A Study of Organizational Adaptation to Environmental Pressures: The Demand for Equal Educational Opportunity.* (Unpublished doctoral dissertation, University of California, January, 1965). Dr. Ball is now Coordinator of Instructional Project Development, Berkeley Unified School District.

**Spurgeon Avakian, *The Politics of Educational Change: Berkeley as Case History.* Unpublished lecture, May 1966.

behaves in Berkeley, and to exhort them to behave likewise. The policy of briefing gave way as the committee was overwhelmed by great numbers of "new" Negroes—many of them poor and undereducated—who began to pour in from the South and the northern cities.

In the past Berkeley has been characterized as conservative, economically self-sufficient, culturally ingrown. In 1947 a contemporary writer stated:

> While there is no political machine in the accepted sense of the phrase, there is nevertheless . . . a ruling group of businessmen, particularly merchants and real estate dealers, whose primary concern is city taxes, as is that of the local newspaper. . . . In general this group has provided conservative, honest, and efficient government, but the government services have been limited because the *primary concern of the group has been to maintain a low tax rate rather than to provide for the needs of the community.* [Italics mine.]

This ruling group has been predominantly Republican, although since 1947 opposition candidates have been elected to the city council and local Democrats have been actively engaged in attempting to change the image of the conservative community. Citizen opposition to school bond issues was persistent.

Since 1926 eleven bond elections were held within the school district and only two passed. The last one barely squeaked through in 1962, the fourth time around. Schools were only reluctantly and parsimoniously financed.

How does the process of change take place? Why is Berkeley, once typical of comfortable smaller cities, now facing up to the educational needs of all its children? We are constantly asked, "How do you begin to integrate?" I answer "You begin with a good school board, one that believes that integration is necessary." First, you get one committed member and he brings in others—or perhaps he makes a dent in the convictions of one or two old members. Then you get a school superintendent committed to bringing integration about. In Berkeley this process began in 1956, moved ahead, was stalled, went ahead again. Judge Avakian describes the changes in the Berkeley schools over the past 10 years as "a tremendous revolution, yet one accomplished without the usual demonstrations or strikes or at the point of a gun." The change came through evolution, but the extent of change has been truly revolutionary.

The school board of 1956 was conservative, oriented toward the business community, and dominated by conservative Republicans. The *Berkeley Daily Gazette* reflected the attitudes of school board and establishment. The board heard only the community's main desire—to keep taxes down. Its school superintendent for 11 years kept school taxes down and kept the sterile peace.

"Although he had an administrative advisory council to discuss projects and programs, the superintendent himself made all major decisions," Dr. Ball reports. Teachers had no formal contact with him. Informal communication was also limited. Those who got his ear did not discuss educational matters with him. Apparently he found it difficult to join in the sharing of ideas, especially liberal ideas on education. His friends were generally Republican, conservative and Caucasian, members of downtown service and business clubs, and especially fellow outdoor sports enthusiasts. Those who camped, hunted, and fished with him found this outwardly austere man a warm individual with whom they could communicate more freely, and Ball says, "the hunters were key figures in the organizational structure."

Rumbles of discontent began to be heard. Early in 1956 individuals and groups who were fed up with the board's lack of response to the total community began to protest and organize. The teachers had always been poorly paid because the administration could draw on the large supply of University graduates and students' wives at low salaries. Teachers pressed in vain for a salary increase. The answer was always "No, no money." At this time the board was threatened by the prospect of losing a 35-cent city tax. Meanwhile the teachers took matters into their own hands, and joined by individuals and groups who shared their demand for change, they got a proposal on the ballot for a 50-cent tax increase to be used to increase salaries and reduce class size. Belatedly and cautiously, the board passed a motion indicating it would appreciate passage of the teachers' measure. The teachers' group worked strenuously and successfully pushed both tax proposals through.

This unprecedented victory encouraged the organization of The Committee on the Berkeley Schools, committed to changing the status quo. And a board election was coming up. Although it was initially made up of teachers and hill liberals, the committee rapidly developed into a cross-section of the whole community, including Negroes. The committee developed a crusading fervor, and took equal opportunity for education as one of its goals. It worked to change the board, to elect a member who shared its commitment. The members chose Dr. Paul Sanazaro. Next election he swept an incumbent out of office by a two-to-one vote.

The old members of the board had never heard of Sanazaro; they did not move in his circles. Dr. Sanazaro, a native of the Bay Area, had been a prize student at Berkeley's Garfield Junior High School, at Berkeley High School, and at the University of California and he led his class at U. C. Medical School in San Francisco. He lived in Berkeley and taught at the University medical school where repeatedly he was voted best teacher of the year. Avakian calls him a man with a most brilliant mind—"a tremendous diagnostician, both medically and educationally." He was always able to ask the right questions, Avakian said, to face community facts, define issues, and force a confrontation. He was the first board member with a different philosophy—the philosophy of change.

The NAACP, led by the Reverend Roy Nichols, had actively worked for Sanazaro's election. Now, the NAACP pressed hard and articulately for change. The percentage of Negro pupils was more than one-fourth (28.7 per cent) of the school population. The first "Statement of the Committee on the Berkeley Schools and the Berkeley NAACP,"* presented by the Reverend Nichols, pointed out the traditional racial division of the city into white hills and Negro flats. The city must recognize that Berkeley schools were segregated schools. Change would not be easy. He cited the "fusion schools" (one Berkeley High School, mainly Negro Burbank Junior High School, the mixture of races at Willard Junior High School) to which students come from racially separated schools in the Negro community, poorly prepared because of cultural or educational unreadiness. High transiency among both students and teachers, latent prejudice, teacher inadequacies, disciplinary problems, and family breakdowns complicated the situation.

> We are sympathetically aware that school administrators, under these circumstances, are "hard put." But here, within the shadow of one of the world's greatest universities, we have our resources, we have intelligence, we have unlimited possibilities for cooperation.
>
> We have heard of the Springfield Plan, the St. Louis Plan, the Washington Plan. *What is the Berkeley Plan?*
>
> We want to help. But you must set forth the program that we may do so with intelligence. We want to cooperate. But we must be told the facts. . . . Our concern is not for the present alone. We know well that this area of the Pacific

* Ball, pp. 32-37.

Coast has only begun to see the population groundswell about to descend upon us. Most of it will come from the South and the Far West. In some respects, our task is as difficult as Little Rock's. *We are here to learn how we can help.*

"What can we do to help?"—that was the clincher. "Nothing"—that was the answer. The board members saw no evidence of serious racial tensions in the schools; furthermore the problems were mainly *within* races rather than between them; the school system would continue to handle its inner problems wisely, realizing it has no control over—or responsibility for—what happens away from the schools after school hours; parents involved could cooperate with the schools to handle any problems. Let the Committee and the NAACP go away now and leave the board to its business. Let a representative of the NAACP meet with the secondary principals to discuss the questions raised—to find out if a citizens' committee was really needed.

The traditional Old Berkeley attitude was still very much alive. "Our" Negroes, the "old" residents, are traditionally "good" Negroes. They behave respectfully and respectably. The "new" incoming Negroes may be different, but are they really our problem? It is the old Negro Berkeleyans' responsibility to set things straight for Negroes who get out of line. The board, however, had a hard time categorizing the NAACP. The NAACP belonged to both. Polished, scholarly, politically progressive, the Reverend Nichols could be labeled an old Negro only in terms of residence; he could scarcely be called a good Negro who would keep quiet about inequities.

The NAACP pressed on. Six months later it had influenced the board to "make a study." The Advisory Committee to Study Certain Racial Problems in the Berkeley Schools and Their Effect on the Community was appointed in June, 1958, headed by Judge Redmond C. Staats. Its report, known as the Staats Report, was the beginning of the end of the old era. Earlier in the year the superintendent and chief spokesman for the old era announced his decision to retire. The forces for change were gaining momentum.

Now came the search for his successor. The board announced that it was looking for a man who could win forthcoming bond elections for the schools. Privately board members wanted to find someone who could bring about better communication and personal relations with the staff.

The man they chose, C. H. Wennerberg, Superintendent of Schools in Whittier, California, was outstanding. As superintendent of the Whittier school system for nine years, he had developed one of the most rapidly expanding secondary school systems in California. He was as communicative, warm and outgoing as the old superintendent had been closed mouthed and cold. He was a political liberal. He had grown up with and taught minority groups, mainly the Mexican-American, and understood their problems.

When Wennerberg came, he saw many problems to attack. Writing about them later, he listed deteriorated guidance services; stress at the high school level only upon academic classes; a school organization isolated from parents and community; an organization where hidden agendas were a way of life; school plants that due to previous economy measures met neither the standards of safety or efficiency.

He put to work his philosophy of communication and sharing. He believed in democratic leadership, with the superintendent acting as catalyst toward consensus. Authority was delegated to staff members able to take the responsibility. Staff decisions were made as a group.

Into this new climate came the startling Staats Report on "Interracial Problems and Their Effect on Education in the Public Schools of Berkeley, California," presented on October 19, 1959. The inequities of Berkeley's Little Rock were now exposed, along with suggested methods of change.

The segregated housing pattern, whites in the hills, Negroes and other minorities in the flats, reflected in ghetto schools.

Inadequate, insufficient, and discriminatory counseling.

Among 560 teachers, only 36 Negroes and those not assigned to a predominantly white school unless requested by parents at that school—or until there is a sufficient nucleus of Negro pupils; need for teacher understanding of the special needs of minority children

Need for Negro history and the Negro's contributions to be included in curriculum

Grouping ("tracking") that results in segregation and isolation of Negro students

Lack of sufficient communication with parents

Behavior problems, although no open conflict in the schools, show Negro juveniles' arrests proportionately high

In the 1959 school board election Spurgeon Avakian, a local attorney, won one of the two vacancies and joined Dr. Sanazaro as a fighting liberal. Now there were two liberals to three conservatives. Then one conservative resigned, and the situation was two-to-two. From 1959-1961 a stalemate prevailed, 18 months of division and marking time. They could not agree on an appointee to fill out the unexpired term so that seat was vacant for eight months. In 1960 the issue of appointing a new member exploded when two teachers, cited by the State House Un-American Activities Committee, were fired. One teacher was up for tenure, the other one year away from tenure. The Alameda County Distrcit Attorney assumed, and wrote that neither one should be rehired. One teacher was professionally unsatisfactory, and all board members accepted this decision. The two conservatives wanted to fire the other teacher too, but the two liberals held out for no dismissal without facts. The conservatives would not budge from their stand and insisted that only a person who would promise to fire the teacher should be named to the board. Both teachers were fired but no one was named to fill the vacancy on the board. Both sides were adamant. The issue got so hot that a public meeting was held. The stamping and shouting of the 1,000 citizens rocked the Community Theater.

A public election followed on the heels of this emotional impasse. Another resignation left two vacancies on the board. Two liberals were elected, a smashing endorsement of the need for change. Four liberals to one conservative on the Berkeley school board in 1961.

"Great things were now to happen."

In 1962 a bond election finally won, by 67 per cent of the votes. The victory came only after a tremendously strenuous campaign against the strong opposition of the status quo Berkeley Citizens United. Now the new board could begin to move more rapidly against the inequities exposed by the Staats Report.

During the spring of 1962, two representatives of the local chapter of the Congress of Racial Equality (CORE) burst into the administrative office demanding to see the superintendent. Hearing the commotion, the superintendent invited the two men into his office to hear their charge that the district was failing to meet the needs of Negro students. They were taken aback when the superintendent agreed that de facto segregation did indeed exist within the district. More than that, they learned of the progress the district had made and were invited to report their questions and suggestions to the board.

On May 1, 1962, CORE made its presentation to the

board. It asked for (1) recognition that segregation did exist, (2) agreement that it should be eliminated, and (3) the appointment of a committee to study the problem and plan to remedy the situation. The first two steps, as CORE knew by this time, had been taken, some changes had been made, but the board agreed with the proposal for a new and sharper study. The Board referred the matter to Superintendent Wennerberg to study over the summer. That fall the superintendent recommended that CORE's basic recommendations be accepted, and the Citizens' Committee on De Facto Segregation was born. Over 130 nominations were submitted by individuals and organizations. The 36 chosen for the committee represented the entire city. The committee's duties were to determine the extent of de facto segregation, to investigate the effects of such segregation on the children, and to bring the findings, conclusions, and recommendations to the board. The board saw in the committee the means of change—where projects, plans, and policies that had been previously stalled in the bureaucracy of the old school establishment would be brought to light. This committee, called the Hadsell Committee after its chairman, Dr. John S. Hadsell, Presbyterian campus minister, worked diligently through most of 1963 and presented its report in November of that year.

The report struck the community like a bombshell. It recommended desegregating the junior high schools by assigning some students from the predominantly Caucasian hill area to Burbank, the Negro junior high school; some of the students from Burbank would be assigned to Garfield, the Caucasian junior high school. The third junior high school already was racially balanced. This recommendation would have eliminated de facto segregation at the junior high school level. Although the community was aware that the committee was functioning, most people had not seriously believed that a concrete recommendation would be made. The reaction was intense. During the remainder of 1963 and through January of 1964 there was extensive community discussion of the proposal. Two hearings were held—one attracting 1,200 people and another drawing over 2,000. PTA's and other groups set up study committees on this problem; never before had such crowds attended PTA meetings.

Many hill liberals faced a dilemma. "How do we express our opposition to this particular proposal without sounding like bigots?" The school board's response was to ask them to develop a better plan. Many critics of the proposal were sincere and set out to do just that.

One of these alternative proposals was the Ramsey Plan, named after the junior high school English teacher who suggested it. This plan proposed desegregation of Berkeley's three junior high schools by making the predominantly Negro school into a ninth grade school and dividing the seventh and eighth graders between the two remaining junior high schools.

In February, 1964, a five-member staff committee was asked to study the reactions of the Berkeley school staff to the citizens committee proposal and to other ideas that had been offered. Every school faculty was asked to consider the matter. In March the committee reported to the board that the staff as a whole was favorable toward integration and preferred the Ramsey Plan to the original citizens committee proposal. The board instructed the superintendent to consider the pros and cons of the Ramsey Plan from the standpoint of educational goals and whether it could be put into effect the following fall.

The results of his study were presented to the board and the community on May 19, 1964, a landmark in the history of Berkeley schools. Again there were over 2,000 people in the audience. The opposition, which had formed the Parents Association for Neighborhood Schools

(PANS), solemnly warned that if the Ramsey Plan or any such desegregation proposal were adopted, the board would face a recall election. The board members voted for the Ramsey Plan—and they did face recall.

During all of this turmoil the board was busy trying to find a successor to Superintendent Wennerberg, who had resigned to continue his doctoral studies at the University. He had fought the battle well. His commitment, courage, vitality, and warm personality had won him many friends and supporters. During his six-year term, backed by the board's liberal majority, he had paved the way for the progress Berkeley is making now. Introducing him at his last official speech—at the Berkeley High School graduation exercises in June, 1964—the Reverend Roy Nichols, then board president, pointed to 13 areas of accomplishment made by the retiring superintendent, all leading up to the biggest job of all, the beginning of the end of de facto segregation.

This is the heady Berkeley mixture I became part of in the fall of 1964. School board member Spurgeon Avakian had sought me out in Prince Edward County. Then I came to Berkeley to meet the other board members and case the situation. I knew they wanted me to provide quality education, as good if possible as that in Old Westbury, Long Island, one of the richest districts in the nation, where I had been superintendent.

Personally, I was determined to move only to a school system where my Prince Edward involvement could continue. Prince Edward County was a part of me that I would not discard or diminish. I wanted to make sure that I could be myself, that I could express my own social philosophy, not be just an administrator and a figurehead. Traditionally and almost universally across the country, school superintendents have been expected to be quiet fellows, keeping their mouths shut on local, national, and world controversial issues. But I am not a quiet fellow. I'm tired of turning over the great problems of the world to haber-dashers, druggists, and generals. I want to speak out on human problems, on civil rights. I feel that is a school administrator's duty.

I felt that the Berkeley board members wanted my total personal and professional self—my commitment to integration, the skills I had developed over 30 years in education, my desire to innovate and change, and my readiness to act—to act politically. Judge Avakian's later remarks bore this out.

"It's not true that schools should stay out of politics," Avakian said. "It's not true that schools should maintain a tranquil atmosphere, thereby keeping things the way they are and the way they always have been. Political involvement develops a meaningful majority, which is essential to gain the consent of the governed." The community must support change. It must protect the schools from those who stand opposed to change. The Board of Education must be the tool of change, openminded rather than doctrinaire. Its members must be willing to preserve change instead of the status quo; they must provide leadership, involve the community, *and run the risk.*

The board should know what the community needs. It should also find out what the community wants and will accept, but not in order to figure out how the public will vote. Community relationships, community peace are not the goals of the board. Education *is* the goal. When people are unhappy, is the problem to make them friendly? Or is it to recognize the source of their discontent and give their children the right kind of education? The administrator too has the obligation to strike out for reform. "Administrators must be bold and courageous," said Avakian. "Mostly, they are not. The able administrator who sticks his neck out will get better results. If he gets his head chopped off, he will be in great demand elsewhere."

I have spoken out in Berkeley—against the Viet Nam

war, against the tragic cuts in domestic programs, against suppression of dissent, against California's Committee on Un-American Activities when it attacked the University and our public schools, against the California Department of Public Instruction for its bureaucratic ambiguity, its fumbling inadequacy, its stifling of innovation, its lack of support for desegregation. And I have been welcome here in Berkeley where the problems, as John Miller said, are, in fine, the problems of the world, and where we recognize that fact.

6

Out of the Frying Pan

I DID NOT COME TO BERKELEY with blind idealistic zeal. Nor did I come seeking a rest, although my wife and I could have used one. After a year in Prince Edward County, Virginia, I was painfully aware of what I was up against. That had been a remarkable year—packed with action, danger, a certain amount of legitimate fear, a great deal of love and friendship, and much satisfaction in accomplishment.

My wife Martha and I moved into a rented home outside Farmville, Virginia, in the summer of 1963. In 1959, Prince Edward County had closed its public schools rather than desegregate them as the Supreme Court mandate required. White children attended private "academies"; Negro youngsters stayed home. President John F. Kennedy and Attorney General Robert Kennedy had taken a personal interest in the case and, as a result of their concern, I had been appointed to set up and administer the Free School Association.

The story of that historic year has been told many times. The Free Schools were opened by a dedicated interracial staff made up of all the committed educators I could hastily recruit, with or without credentials. I asked only that my teachers possess a desire to teach these children, a true non-do-gooder love for them, and understanding and skill. Negro children numbering 1,567, many of them

[4 7]

afraid even to speak, let alone to read, entered the classroom for the first time in four years.

The story of my family's personal education has not been told as often. I had taken a year's leave from my superintendency in comfortable, wealthy, all-white East Williston, Long Island, where quality academic education could easily be achieved. In Farmville, we moved into the local hotel and set out to rent a home. The lunatic fringe went into action right away, making sleep impossible for us at the hotel, by telephoning every hour from midnight to 6 a.m. When we told the switchboard operator not to put through any calls, the operator would tell us a hospital was calling, that one of our sons had been injured. This would force us to accept the call.

After weeks of searching, two houses were offered us. Negotiations on one broke down as soon as they learned that we were Catholics. The second offer, which we hastily accepted, had been made, we later learned, only after three weeks of soul-searching by the owner with her minister. The rent was accordingly high. In spite of an unlisted phone number, our persecution had only begun. Now the fanatic segregationists came in person. Almost every night cars would speed through our large curving driveway, horns blasting. When the raiders tired of this game, they came at night and dumped garbage in the driveway, later on the steps, then on the veranda.

The games followed a pattern. When there was court action on the Prince Edward County School case, we had many night visitors; when there was a quiet period, harassment fell off. Bomb threats came more frequently when court action warmed up. My wife and I began sleeping in separate rooms. We figured that if a bomb went off our sons would have at least one parent left. Well, we didn't get a bomb, but one night a car drove up and a great blast shook the house. I recognized it as a 10-gauge, double-barreled shotgun. What did I do? I dived under the bed.

We had a little peace after President Kennedy's assassination. There was a great wave of guilt so tangible you could feel it. This lasted through the holiday season but after the first of the year our night callers renewed their visits. But now they changed their gifts—they raided the cemeteries for funeral wreaths and left them at our door and around the house.

The only real welcome we got came from the Negroes and the very small Catholic church. The white Protestant church avoided me like the plague. Its members did not dare invite me to meet with them or attend their services. The black Protestant church went out of its way to invite me and to make me feel at home. The little Catholic church had a remarkable parish priest. He was young, vibrant, committed to integration, and was one of the great people I met in the county. He not only made me feel at home but he also had a handful of Catholic blacks who attended Mass regularly and were great supporters of mine.

We were cut off from all the kinds of social life we had known in the white society, and much of the Negro community was afraid to take us into their midst. Fear prevailed, even in the classroom. The Negro children were afraid to come near us. When Martha and I drove out to their homes, the children ran and hid. Their mothers refused to come to the door.

But as the year went on all this changed. By spring, when we rode through the Negro section the youngsters and their parents ran out to meet us. We were no longer whites, the enemy. We were teachers and friends. This was the wonderful and direct benefit of the Free Schools.

By year's end, when the Supreme Court in May, 1964, ordered Prince Edward County to open its schools to all children my assignment was completed. I was sorry to leave Prince Edward. It had been a great experience. From a professional standpoint, never had I seen so much accomplished in so short a time. How had it been accomplished? By money—government money, Kennedy Foundation money, other foundation money. By bringing together all county, state, and federal resources. By hiring an integrated staff, all committed to one purpose—equal opportunity to learn. We packed three years' reading into one; we prepared Negro teenagers for college; we took them out into the world to learn they could be part of it; we erased fear.

After such a year, I could not go back to comfortable Old Westbury, although I had been very happy with its achievement of high quality education. Nor could I accept other posts I had been offered.

I wanted to carry on, to go forward. I wanted to go to a school district where there was a fighting chance to win desegregation and to work with a school board committed to this goal. Berkeley was the place. The answer had to be Yes. In Berkeley the struggle had begun.

True, the Berkeley setting was quite different from Farmville, Virginia. It was easy to rent a house—and to buy one, if you could find the $40-, $50-, or $60,000 to pay for it. I could certainly entertain Negroes in my home, although I might not find many hill neighbors doing the same. Nobody would strew garbage in my yard or come after me with a double-barreled shotgun. But the basic attitude was the same—only more polite. Negro children lived in the ghetto and went to ghetto schools; white hill parents, even those who proclaimed their support for integration, clung to their neighborhood all-white schools; and most parents—upper-, middle-, and lower middle-class— were opposed to elementary desegregation, which meant busing. I needed an unlisted telephone in my home in Berkeley. In my office the flood of fanatic phone calls would pour in as desegregation moved ahead. And on my desk the poison-pen letters would pile up.

During the late spring and summer of 1964, as my family prepared to move, things were happening fast. Following the board's May 19 adoption of junior high school desegregation, the opponents obtained enough signatures to force a recall election. Of the five-member Board of Education which had unanimously invited me to come to Berkeley, only two remained in office. Still in office to face the recall election were Mrs. Carol R. Sibley, widow of a distinguished U. C. professor and a civic leader in her own right, and Professor Sherman Maisel of U. C. (Dr. Maisel has since become a Governor of the Federal Reserve Board.)

The Friends of the Berkeley Schools, made up of pro-integration citizens of all races, was formed to defend the board against the recall threat. Following a series of procedural skirmishes before the city council and the state courts, the recall election was scheduled for October 6.

On September 1, 1964—five weeks before the recall election—I took office as Berkeley's Superintendent of Schools. In the midst of this climate of change and uncertainty, with virtually an entirely new administration and a mostly new board (its three vacancies filled by the board until the next city election) it was our task to open schools under the Ramsey Plan—and to show that the world would not come to an end with the desegregation of the secondary schools. We were successful.

One of my first public appearances was at a night rally at new West Campus by the Friends of the Berkeley Schools, and I looked over the schoolground audience. Many had come in a parade of cars—a parade that had passed almost unnoticed through the quiet streets. The rally was not large. Who were these people? They looked like the sturdy battlers for progress—the liberals, many of them Negroes, the proponents of change in a city that had long held out against it.

Did these people represent the majority vote? Where were the so-called nice people, the first of our limited hill supporters, the middle-of-the-roaders, the staunch Berkeley old ladies? Snug in their homes, no doubt. (Well, it was a cool, windy evening.)

Where were the members of the establishment? Probably at a PANS meeting.

Where was the press? Not visible.

I could not really tell much about the strength of my support that night. How far would I be allowed to go on my commitment to integration? Both elected board members, of course, were back of me. The other three were interim appointees, who would have to run for election the next April. I could count on former board members, but their help was limited. Avakian, now a Superior Court judge, was back of me, but he was not free to participate now that he was on the bench. The Reverend Nichols had come back from his new post as minister to a large congregation in New York City to lend his voice for integration, but he would have no Berkeley vote.

As the hammering and blasting for recall went on in the *Berkeley Daily Gazette,* I continued to wonder. Then the answer: a NO to recall on October 6 by 61 per cent of the approximately 40,000 who voted. It was a stunning triumph for the courageous incumbent board members. There was more at stake, however, than individual board members continuing in office. A Board of Education had voluntarily taken effective action to desegregate schools— not because of court order or other compulsion, but simply due to their commitment. If "liberal" Berkeley would not allow this board to survive, the lesson would not be lost in other cities facing the same problem. Thus, it was extremely significant that the board and its action were vindicated by the Berkeley community.

Now the board could settle down to the business of

running the schools—the two veterans, no longer beleaguered, and the three interim appointees—Dr. Samuel A. Schaaf, a University of California professor and chairman of the Department of Mechanical Engineering; John J. Miller, an attorney and a Negro; and the Reverend Laurence P. Byers, a Presbyterian minister. All were liberal, all favored integration; soon enough they could be targets again when the regular school election came up in the spring.

On January 26, 1965, the Council of Civic Unity of San Francisco, at its twentieth anniversary dinner, presented its annual Civic Unity award to the Berkeley Board of Education. Carol Sibley and Sherman Maisel, "the only two ducks left to shoot at," received the honor. Mrs. Sibley, board president, shared the honors given to her and Dr. Maisel with former board members—Reverend Nichols and Judge Avakian, as well as with former Berkeley School Superintendent Wennerberg. She also gave me credit for my consultation with the board at intervals during the preceding spring and summer which, she said, "helped immeasurably to get the Ramsey Plan off to an excellent, carefully thought-out start."

She called what had happened in the Berkeley schools "the history in a nutshell of one community that dared to face its problems and to try to build true community confidence and trust." She shared the citation with "the majority of Berkeley voters, the wonderful lay citizen committees that worked so indefatigably on the Staats and Hadsell reports, former Superintendent Wennerberg, NAACP and CORE, who suggested the studies of Berkeley's problems, the school task force, the Friends of the Berkeley Schools, and the teachers, counselors and administrators who have worked with devotion and enthusiasm to implement the new policy."

Carol was in her usual high spirits that night—as always, never indicating any hurts from battle wounds, never maligning her enemies. And Sparky Avakian was his warm and happy self: "Bitter as I felt over the recall attempt, although as a Judge I was not involved; bitter as I was over the race issue, in retrospect I think this whole painful interval has been good for Berkeley. It has laid the foundations for future progress."

The judge could get over his bitterness. Many persons and groups concerned in the recall attempt could not, at least not immediately. West Campus, the ninth grade school, got off to a good start, but at Garfield Junior High School parents feared and resented any change affecting the high academic standards of their school. Many of the parents had been involved in the recall. Our troubles there were far from ended with rejection of recall.

Desegregation—the first steps—had won. Now let the wounds heal; bring the community together for the quality education in which Berkeley believed. Now I went to work on what I called "new directions" to "make Berkeley's schools worthy of imitation." I outlined 17 tasks for the school district in the widely-read national "Letter for Administrators" in the May, 1965, issue of *Educator's Dispatch*. These were, and are, the most important eight steps:

> Promote *positive integration* among races
> Strengthen the reading program
> Make both elementary and secondary schools ungraded
> Develop team teaching
> Explore the advantages of shared services with the non-public schools
> Provide compensatory education from the nursery schools through adulthood
> Find ways to eliminate boredom and fear from the classroom
> Involve students, parents, and public in the quest for solutions to all educational problems

We—the board, the administration, the total staff, the parents—went to work.

I set about to get to know the total community. I met all 700 teachers in our schools in informal dialogues with them at every school. I took part in a weekend conference of 150 staff members—the subject, as the reader might guess, "New Directions in the Berkeley Schools." I held lunch meetings with student leaders at a number of schools. I went into the schools and taught reading, which was so stimulating and so much fun that a number of my fellow administrators did the same. I met with community leaders on educational problems.

I had my secretaries personally call, and I wrote letters to literally hundreds of citizens inviting them to come into my office in small groups and chat with me about public education. Hundreds of them accepted the invitation.

I made speeches wherever I was asked, always on immediate needs of the Berkeley schools, often on integration, often on reading. I was always available to interviewers from the press, ranging from *The Berkeley Barb* on through the more respectable newspapers—white, Negro, Oriental, and Catholic. I wrote articles. I criticized textbook publishers for emphasizing middle-class, Caucasian culture at the expense of minority children. I accepted the invitation to write a weekly column for the *Berkeley Daily Gazette* to make citizens aware of our school programs, to brainstorm too with the community, and to mend fences that had been damaged by the recall controversy. (The *Gazette*, at that time, was beginning to change its tune after the recall defeat.)

We changed the bi-monthly board meeting schedule and held every other meeting at a school, including all the school neighborhoods, instead of the old pattern of holding all meetings at the Administration Building. We urged the public to air their gripes and suggestions there, and by putting their complaints and ideas on the agenda we began to get interested audiences and much stimulating discussion. We set up a School Master Plan Committee of 135 members, a cross-section of the community nominated by the public to consider immediate and long-range plans for the schools.

Because I feel that reading is the most important subject, the key to learning and to integration, I asked the principals of all schools to double or triple the class time devoted to it, even at the expense of other subjects. We provided reading specialists. I said, "Every teacher must be a reading teacher. If he or she does not feel qualified, let that teacher take time to learn." I encouraged the use of every method and every mixture of methods that had been tested and found to work. I don't care if it's phonics, "look-see," or "i/t/a" (a method based on an improvised 44 character phonic alphabet invented in England 100 years ago by Ben Pittman of shorthand fame and adapted by his son for current use.) I could write reams about our home-made reading curriculum, our teaching of English as a second language, made possible in ghetto schools by Federal Elementary and Secondary Education Act-Title I funds.

We in the administration, supported by innovative principals and teachers, urged the production of home-made books by teachers of early grades and the children themselves. It was in this context that I so strongly criticized the textbook publishers—the majority of them—as "a perpetuating force in racial discrimination." During my first winter in Berkeley (1964-1965), the district's Intergroup Education Project held a Community Assembly on Negro History which received national publicity. It drew 700 people from all over California and the Southwest and brought publishers' representatives flying out from New York in a first attempt to mend their ways. The few pioneer interracial textbook ventures on display at the assembly ranged from fairly good models to the primitive black-inking of a few of the youngsters playing with Dick and Jane in the "look-see" books. I said to that assembly that "for all our school children know about Negro history and Negro contributions to our society, they might as well be in Mississippi."

I made speeches and wrote magazine articles in which I took apart the structure of state government in relation to education—its "ambiguous roles, confusion, buck-passing, jockeying for position, time-wasting," causing the legislature to spend hours and hours on such minutiae as determining how many minutes a day should be spent on physical education. I urged that the State Superintendent of Public Instruction be an appointive office rather than a political, elective one. The office should be available to the best qualified educator rather than restricted to educators willing—and financially able—to conduct an intensive statewide campaign.

I was free to speak out. I had the usual contract as superintendent, but I also had the unusual understanding with my board that what I might want to say in public was up to me. I talked about innovation, and my slogan was "Schools worthy of imitation."

I did not talk about the Ramsey Plan. Let it get started, work quietly within the system toward its success. Let the community, which, through its strong vote against the recall of the board, had reinforced the plan, get accustomed to it. Let the losers—the local press, the establishment—recover their balance. For me to have spoken out in praise that first year would only have created more friction. So against my nature, I was silent about the Ramsey Plan. But I was the new superintendent, the man now in charge of the Ramsey Plan, and the public did not keep quiet about me or about the plan I headed. Here are some quotes from a survey made of property owners who threatened to move away from Berkeley because of the new steps in integration and some of whom did move away: "The Berkeley schools can go straight to hell." "Dump Sullivan and use his salary to benefit the families who are the main support of the tax role." "Get rid of Sullivan; cut down on spending."

"I am not satisfied with Dr. Sullivan's program. I respect his achievement in a privately-financed school project in Prince Edward County, but it does not seem wise or profitable to operate on the same basis here . . . Schools in Berkeley cannot cure our social ills." . . . "Keep the niggers by themselves in their own district, their own schools, under their own roofs. I do not believe in pollution of the white race with black blood." "Move the school board to Russia." "I gave up on Berkeley . . . and sent my child to parochial school. They (the Berkeley schools) stink!" "Children should not be made guinea pigs to put a feather in the cap of the Board of Education."

Add to these quotes the many poison-pen letters and the many phone calls I received calling me everything from politely insulting epithets to "nigger-lover." Dump Sullivan, they said. Get rid of him and his ideas. Send him back to Prince Edward County.

The sturdy supporters of the Ramsey Plan stayed with me—a courageous band. The first year would be full of troubles, but we and the plan would survive. The public remark made by an Oakland educator who lives in Berkeley stays with me: "You've gone out on a limb," he said. "You've done things other towns hadn't the nerve to do." The limb was strong, however. At times it shook a bit and sometimes the foxes barked threateningly below. But we hung on.

7

Integration Begins in Berkeley

SEPTEMBER, 1964. It was a Berkeley first for approximately 3,000 secondary school students. It also was a first for the city's ninth-graders, who now had their own campus. It was a first in integration for seventh-graders entering Garfield Junior High School in North Berkeley and for eighth-graders who had attended Garfield the previous year when it was still an almost totally white school.

But in many respects this fall was like every other fall in Berkeley: young people eager to go back to school in September, and most parents very happy to have them go. That was the way it was, to a major extent, at West Campus, the ninth grade school, formerly Burbank Junior High, where parents had expressed little opposition to the plan. Negro students, who had attended seventh and eighth grades there had found it a good ghetto school. Its staff had been dedicated and cohesive. It was easy to return as ninth-graders. They, and their parents, had a vested interest in the success of "Old Burbank" as new West Campus. And parents of white students entering the school had always known that their children would be in a physically desegregated school, Berkeley High School, formerly grades 9-12, at this grade level. But Garfield Junior High School did not have the usual atmosphere of exuberant anticipation that year.

At West Campus there was plenty of room; there were plenty of teachers. The Burbank principal—a warm and strong leader—stayed on. The plant had been renewed and expanded. Many teachers were accustomed to teaching Negro children and the majority of them believed in integration and felt their students would achieve better in the company of Caucasians. New young teachers, interested in experiment and alive to change, had joined the staff and morale was high. But the main reason West Campus was so successful had nothing to do with race. Its success was as much bound up with the psychology of Gesell and Ilg as with the Berkeley Ramsey Plan. The students were all 14 years old—the Negroes, the whites, the Orientals, the Mexican-Americans. They were free from competition with the youth of upper high school grades, who had reached another stage of growth and sophistication. They did not have to be self-conscious about the braces on their teeth, pimply complexions, boys' changing voices that suddenly turned girlish and squeaky, or the plumpness and awkwardness that suddenly—within months—emerges into slimness and grace as children magically start growing up instead of across. Here at West Campus, unlike Berkeley High, overly plump girls or girls with braces on their teeth could be pompon girls; boys with changing voices could sing in the chorus. Group dating was the most comfortable way to socialize, and even though some more mature girls might have preferred older boys to date, there were no older boys around so they made do with those handy.

The principal recognized the needs of this age group and expanded extra-curricular activities, especially dramatics. "This is the 'Who am I?' age," he said. "The kids are trying out roles, seeking self-identity. Dramatics provides a stage—a place to experiment, act out their dreams, find themselves."

The students had a newspaper of their own, a supplement to the high school's rather famous *Jacket,* the only high school daily in the country. Every student had a wide choice of activities; everybody could participate in something interesting beside classes. Both races at West Campus felt they had high status. It was a new socio-educational climate. A survey of the first year of the Ramsey Plan found that 55 per cent of West Campus students liked school better than they had liked it the year before. I thought this was highly significant because the year before most of them had also liked their schools very much.

At Garfield, however, many students and teachers were still affected, and infected by the ideas that formed the basis of the opposition to the Ramsey Plan and the recall. Parents' openly expressed prejudice or hostility to changing Garfield was now shared by their children. Many were frightened and insecure because their parents had told them they planned to move away.

For 50 years Garfield had served children of culturally advantaged homes including homes of University of California faculty members, Bay Area physicians, lawyers, and businessmen. Hill Berkeleyans were proud of its history as a status school and one of the first junior high schools in the United States. (Actually, the junior high school program was started at the same time in New York City.)

Now this utopian haven was to be taken away from them to share it with the Negroes, some of whom might have middle- or even upper-middle-class parents but most of whom came from poor and disadvantaged families. Hostility ranged from unconscious bigotry and prejudice ("We and our children have many Negro friends," "We like Negroes but . . .," etc.) to the stereotype expression of open hostility—their children would be endangered by Negro gangs, even that Negroes are born inferior and unable to learn as well as whites. Hill parents' greatest fear in

Berkeley, where intellectuality and scholarliness are so highly treasured, was that their children would not get into the college of their choice.

Some Negro students were not totally happy about the change either. Many would have been happy to stay on at Burbank. Transportation was a problem and an expense many could not afford. Others were truly afraid to emerge from the ghetto and the ghetto school where they had felt at home. This fear would be strengthened by the hostility of Caucasian children of prejudiced parents. Some of the white children were as afraid of the incoming Negro children as the Negroes were afraid of them. Some had grown up thinking Negroes "look mean" and "are mean." They anticipated fighting and stealing, and there was some of both.

Some of the students from both schools had lost many of their friends in the transfer. There *was* a great disparity between the majority of the white students from the hills and the majority of the Negro students from the flats. Understanding one another was difficult. Add to the picture Garfield's overcrowded conditions, putting a strain on both pupils and teachers. Add also the resentment felt by some of the old Garfield teachers who found it hard to adjust. Their pattern was slow to change. In lunchroom and teachers' lounge one would see a large group of white teachers sitting together, a small group of Negro teachers together, and an equally small mixed group whose members called themselves "mongrels" and worked at changing the pattern of the others.

A number of experiences during that first year at integrated Garfield point up the very deep and real problems we faced. A distraught white mother came to the principal's office at the end of the school year to declare that her son had developed more animosity toward Negroes during his one year at the new Garfield than he had felt during his first seven years in an exclusively Caucasian elementary school. She concluded that Berkeley's attempt to integrate races had failed. The principal's conclusions were different, however. "I told her that in my opinion a declaration of failure at that time was premature. My knowledge of her son did not support her conclusion. The boy had been exposed to an important reality. Before coming to Garfield he had lived in a white 'ivory tower'."

The principal had seen the boy gaining many positive experiences with Negroes. He had seen him working well with them in sports, in the orchestra, and in the classroom. "For the first time, however, the boy was meeting culturally disadvantaged children who were not attuned to upper social class graces," said the principal. "And he reported these experiences to his mother. The Negroes he had told her about had not been involved with so-called 'privileged' children before. They were as much awed by Caucasians as Caucasians were by them. They were anxious to see how white faces reacted. Their attempts were crude, often taking the form of tripping, bumping, 'borrowing,' etc.—techniques frequently used by younger children to initiate rapport. If the Caucasian student responded with evidence of racial discrimination, relationships grew worse. If a certain degree of understanding was shown by the Caucasian, the Negro child responded with obvious signs of friendship."

One Garfield student leader interpreted the situation in this way: many underprivileged Negro students, like their white counterparts, are pranksters, not gangsters, as some people want to believe. Some subconsciously, some intentionally, wanted to know more about their white schoolmates who were such a new experience to them. The first few months were exploratory months for all concerned.

"The fear of the unknown can be more destructive of human relationships than reality," said the principal.

"When plans were being made to integrate Garfield, a PTA officer stated at a public meeting that she did not intend to have her boy 'beaten up' every day by Negroes as she asserted was happening to Caucasian children at other integrated schools. Her son came to Garfield despite her fear and was not exposed to any acts more violent than infrequent childish bullying."

The most obvious gains at Garfield the first year were in social education. Debbie, a Negro pupil, was vilified by a four-year-old white boy at the nursery school where she was assisting as part of her homemaking study. He kicked Debbie and said: "You're black; my daddy says you're not American." Debbie's classmates, members of all races, faced the problem together and discussed the ramifications of social ignorance. An Australian classmate came up and told the little boy that she came from Australia and was not American, but that Debbie was born in America and is just as much an American as he is. "Whether the little boy profited from this experience is not as important as the fact that Debbie and most of her 23 Homemaking classmates profited immensely," commented the principal.

Early in the first year, three eighth-grade boys—a small Negro, a tall Caucasian and a medium-sized Oriental—got together and started a Student Relations Council. It was the Negro boy's idea. He had been taunted and harassed by other Negro students because he "hung around with whites" and got along so well with them. The white boy had received similar treatment because he consorted with Negro classmates. The Oriental was simply understanding and concerned. In a short time the council had 50 members who discussed all sorts of problems, ranging from fights and their deeper cause to how to choose records for dances "that everybody wants." The council, with two committed interracial faculty sponsors, launched constructive projects and became a strong force in the school. It became a prototype for other schools in Berkeley, both in and outside the classroom, and a means of effective, spontaneous intergroup education.

You could find changed attitudes or at least calm acceptance from the parents too. Once we heard,

> Because of the fact that Mr. Sullivan has decided to integrate schools at all cost, most of our reliable taxpaying citizens have moved out of this area with their children, who are no doubt the most intelligent segment of Berkeley students. Where does this lead us? To segregation. When all white children move out, Berkeley is left with all Negroes and some Orientals. . . .
>
> People are leaving Berkeley because the school board is tampering with the schools to the point of absurdity. . . .
>
> I am moving away from Berkeley. It's getting too dark for me here. As soon as they (the Negroes) take over Berkeley we can all go bankrupt.

Where are these families now? Still in Berkeley! The property turnover in Berkeley in 1964-1965, first year of the Ramsey Plan, was virtually the same as in 1960, except that there was an increase in population. There was very little change among the school areas. Many 1964-1965 home-buyers said they had moved to Berkeley because of "satisfaction with the public schooling," "the integrated atmosphere," "the high academic standards and the progressive outlook on social problems."

One reply by a Garfield parent reveals new understanding of misplaced concerns: "I have suggested to my children that we move to Orinda [a nearby wealthy suburb]. They refuse and indicate they are very happy with the Berkeley schools. Why don't you ask the kids?"

We did. At Garfield, the survey found, not all of the students liked it that first year, as we knew. Some of the resentment and negative attitudes of veteran Garfield teachers had rubbed off on their students. The seventh-graders, coming fresh from elementary school in hills or flats, said they liked it better than they had liked school the year before. This attitude could reflect, however, simply their satisfaction in transferring from kid school to grown-up school and the increased freedom that it gives. (Age 12, when most children enter junior high school, is doubtless as crucial as age 14, when they step out and up again.)

According to the survey Garfield teachers were generally negative about the Ramsey Plan at the end of its first year. Teachers who had supported the plan in the beginning still favored it, but they found the students' attitudes poor. Although the majority of the students supported the change, almost one-third said they did not like school as well this year.

But these children, just out of elementary, showed a real insight into the reasons their school was now different. Unlike many of the adults affected by the change, they were able to see beyond their own familiar environment and relate their experience to the larger world. They realized that it was perhaps not so important that they like new Garfield. "When asked how they liked the 'new Garfield,' pupils frequently responded that although they were not as comfortable as they might have been with their 'look-alikes' in a segregated situation, they realized that much of the 'comfort' of the segregated schools was superficial."

Now the differences were exposed. Some young people were sufficiently discerning and intelligent to value the "good," interesting, creative differences. Some were sophisticated enough to rationalize them. But most of the Negroes were poor and ghetto-bound; most of the Caucasians were privileged and free. Envy was understandably rampant. The Negro children could not help coveting the clothes, the transistors, the lipsticks, the pocket money, the many gadgets money could buy for the white children.

And the white children, although some understood the envy and felt guilty, wanted to hang on to their possessions. Some gave out of fear or guilt, but none wanted to be forced by threats or violence.

Throughout the years, many Negro children have been brought up to accept the unjust society—the inequality of housing, privileges and possessions; the daily put-down, the daily hurt. They were taught to control their anger, to harden themselves not to feel it, or to bottle it up. To keep them safe, their mothers commanded them every morning, "Don't answer back, don't fight, don't get into trouble." But all parents are not saying this these days, and not all Negro children are willing any longer to accept this pattern of restraint or self-defeat.

C. Elrie Chrite, a juvenile intake supervisor of a detention home in Michigan where many of the youths who exploded during the Detroit riots were incarcerated, spoke to the essence of the changed attitudes of the young Negro.

> When I was growing up, I was taught to rationalize the name-calling. I was told 'don't lower yourself and act in a degrading way because you're called names.'
>
> Youngsters who have come up since the 1954 Supreme Court decision are not afraid. They refuse to accept this kind of treatment for any reason, and society at large is not geared to handle this change in youth.

Of course Berkeley cannot be compared to Ypsilanti or Willow Run or other Detroit area communities where the southern white-Negro bitterness and competition exists. But in the microcosm of Garfield Junior High School, we understood this new awareness and this strong hostility, although we did not condone its expression. We geared ourselves to stick it out—white and black together.

At Garfield, desegregation had been accomplished. The deeper process of integration had begun. The first year had been a rugged one but the next year was 100 per cent better, the third better still, as I shall describe later in this book. Even during that first strenuous year, many good things happened. A moving letter from a Negro girl who had been an elected officer of the Garfield student body best expresses the successes of the first year of our mission of change.

This will be a shock. I can't come back to Garfield. My parents had to move away. Tell the future and past students that I'm very sorry. Tell them if they have a chance to become something good, become it. Please don't give me credit for anything I have done. My teachers gave me the urge to go on; let them urge other people as they did me. I'm very sorry I can't come back.

8

Integration of the Teens—
New Lessons to be Learned

IS IT TOO LATE TO INTEGRATE AT AGES 12, 13, and 14? My answer is Yes, it is too late—too late for some, but better late than never. To most, I would say, it is a therapeutic exposure; although the disease of prejudice and the scars of discrimination, isolation, and fear are far advanced, some victims at least can be cured or healed. But it is a tough and painful process for these teenagers whom we have wronged by not bringing them together as children, before the disease set in.

Let me say, as I see these 12- to 14-year-olds in interaction, it is a breakthrough, an exciting beginning. Integration, however, cannot suddenly be imposed painlessly on students who have lived all their lives in almost all-white or all-Negro neighborhoods and have attended almost all-white or all-black schools, and who have been instilled with the prevailing prejudices, misconceptions and fears.

I want to tell how it looked on the surface in June, 1967, the end of the third year. I shall write mainly about Garfield Junior High School, the formerly prestige white school of tight tradition and upper-class orientation, the school where much of the opposition to integration had centered.

Students were separating for the summer, going their different ways. In Berkeley this means the white students are mostly going up to their homes in the hills, perhaps off

[69]

to camp, and the Negro students are going down to their homes in the ghetto. Some—very few—would meet this summer at parks and swim centers, at hamburger joints where the juke boxes pour out rock 'n roll, at bus stops, and at a very few homes.

In the corridors and on the playground little groups gather. The pattern is mainly all-black and all-white—a Negro group here, a white group there, from which singly or in pairs students cross over to say, almost formally and somewhat self-consciously, "Bye, I'll be seeing you," or whatever phrase is current. There are small mixed groups and they tend to fall into two patterns, signified by their dress. One group, Negro and white alike, is dressed conventionally—the girls in skirts and sweaters, their hair short and carefully groomed; the boys in neat sweaters and slacks. They are to some extent upper middle class but mainly conventional middle class or middle-class oriented. The other group is "far-out" in faddish dress—the girls in miniskirts and boots, their hair long, fantastic earrings dangling from pierced ears; the boys in tight trousers, gaudy shirts or ponchos, their hair down to their eyebrows and shoulders.

Both groups are acting out their attempts at integration. One is staying with the status quo outward pattern, in polite and cautious mixing. The other is going all out in a flamboyant sharing of costume and language, including the use of four-letter words. Among them are the young intellectuals, the committed, the activists, and the rebels— some, all of these. Many of them come from politically liberal families and have been brought up in an atmosphere of concern for social change. They are the ones who at Garfield had joined older students in staging an anti-Viet Nam war rally. They are the adventurous who may try everything. They are attracted by the hippies' venture into a utopian world. They see the contradictions in our society, want to change the world or make one of their own. Their parents are both proud of them and very worried about them.

True, on some school days—when class photographs are being taken, or when parents come visiting and the school is showing off—you will see these same children in neat conventional dress. And on weekends you would see many of them blended into a proper church or temple congregation. At such times they have dropped their masks and their costumes of liberation.

Then there are others—the sullen and apart, scornful, held back from any group, unable to break through.

Children wear many masks and act out many patterns. Many ghetto Negroes have adopted the middle-class mask of constraint in self-expression, neatness and orderliness, obedience to convention, conformity. With some Negroes —a diminishing group, I'm glad to note—this descends into the Uncle Tom pattern imposed in the South and in Old Berkeley when the first migrants came. Others play it safe out of fear or dignity, "act nice" toward whites or ignore their insults as not worth their trouble. There are children, white and Negro, brought up freely and permissively and therefore able to be spontaneous—for better and for worse. There are pranksters, as the principal calls some of the Negro boys and girls who shove and push and pull girls' hair. With some this is a way to get acquainted —a physical means of contact. With others it's just plain hostility. Sometimes, with girls, it's admiration. And of course, it's envy of privileges denied.

There are also gangs. The Negro gangs are more conspicuous, more numerous, and easier to pin down for wrongdoing. White gangs, like the gang of sixth-graders at one hill school, jimmy lockers to steal the contents, unscrew library table legs so the heavy top will fall on the unsuspecting, turn off the electric power, and so on. Society rationalizes this "mischief." The erratic behavior can be explained away by saying that the children probably come from broken homes, or have been too permissively brought up, or are alienated. Then parents send them to psychiatrists at $35-$50 an hour. But what do we do about the Negro gangs? Do we take pains to understand them? Do we look to see if they too may have come from broken homes, that they too are alienated? Can they go to psychiatrists?

At Garfield hostility showed itself in many ways. Some Negro boys and girls pushed and shoved and pulled hair, threatened and chased and shook down white youths for coveted possessions. White boys and girls tended to take out their hostility in caustic wounding words or in isolating themselves from classroom or social contact with their Negro fellow students.

But one important lesson was learned by students of both races—the students who were ready and willing to learn. In every race or group, there is variety; every individual is different. The right to enjoy this individuality, this uniqueness has not been granted to the Negro in our society, however, where the total burdens of his race, the sins and omissions of all are blended into one stereotype imposed upon the individual Negro. At Garfield the students began to learn that Negroes, like whites, come in all shapes, sizes, and personalities.

In general there was considerable hostility among students and between races. The Negro students expressed their feelings more openly, the whites were more inhibited. To some Negro youths, the Garfield situation was a long delayed confrontation of pent-up resentment—"You've been taking it away from us, now we'll take it away from you." But in individual relationships it was clear that hostility was not that implacable, that barriers to understanding were not that high.

Let me tell you about two situations faced by two white girls—girls from liberal families who were committed to making integration work. Jeannie, tall and blonde and flamboyant in dress, became the target of Irene, a small Negro girl who happened to be plain. As Jeannie was applying her new "coral sunset" lipstick, Irene came up and demanded "Give it to me!" Jeannie started to hand it over and avoid trouble, but another Negro girl shouted "Don't!" So Jeannie withheld the lipstick and, for her pains, got chased to her bus and all but caught for a hair-pulling. The next day, when Jeannie saw Irene putting on a new "flaming orange" lipstick, she had an idea. "I'll give you mine if you'll give me yours," she offered. So the two girls swapped and after that there was peace and eventually friendship.

The other incident involved Jeannie's friend Fran. As Fran stood on the school steps—her long hair flowing, gaudy earrings swinging—a Negro boy came along and knocked her books from her arm. Then he looked at her contemptuously and spat on the ground in her direction. "What's the matter with you?" Fran challenged him. "Do you hate me? Do you hate me because I'm white?" The boy stared at her silently for a long moment, then said: "Yeh, I guess that's it." Then he picked up her books and handed them to her, the anger gone from his eyes.

Talking of this confrontation later, Fran said: "The thing is we've got to equal with each other. We've got to quit being afraid of each other. We've got to open up to each other."

Such incidents, I hasten to say, are only part of the picture at Garfield. Among Jeannie's and Fran's new-made friends is Pat, a beautiful bouncy Negro girl who goes around breaking up all-white or all-Negro groups. She also parades the corridors with a different white boy every day. "I'm going to shake you whiteys loose," she says, laughing.

"I'm going to make you *human!*" And there is Pete, the Negro boy who started Garfield's Student Relations Council which meets weekly after school, faces and works out interracial conflicts.

And there is Brenda, a Negro sweater-and-skirt girl, who in the school year 1966-1967 was elected student body president by a 1,055-201 vote. With her in the student governing body are one Negro and two Caucasians. She is a great leader.

Hostility, warmth and friendship, pain and happiness— all go together in this great surfacing, this great opening up we see on our desegregated campuses. Marsha Turner, a Negro student, explained the dichotomy in a little essay in the June, 1966, issue of Garfield's literary magazine "Caesura," published by English students. She calls her essay "Freedom is a Personal Thing." She wrote:

> Sometimes I think that I am divided into two parts—the bitter and the optimistic.
> (The Bitter)
> I am to be hated and to be looked down upon by scum, why shouldn't I hate back? Why shouldn't I seek revenge in hating the white man? Then, as all of this tension is poured upon my people, they scream out, "I want to be seen. I want to have an equal chance. I want to be free!" Free from what? We are no longer in chains, but by the ropes that keep us from getting equal opportunities. The only way that we can have freedom is to fight for it.
> (The Optimistic)
> On my optimistic days, I remind myself that I have found new friends and new interests since I started going to Garfield. The first day, I was unaware of what was going on. The most amazing thing to me was the warmth and the friendliness all children of different colors "dished out" to me. I went to school feeling as though I might not be accepted as a Negro. In my bewilderment, I forgot all about the racial barriers that we cannot see (but know are there)

and began making friends with every glance and every breath. It was a pleasing experience to me. Slowly, I have come out of my shell of shyness and have found many friends and enemies.

My enemies are not what I expected! I expected to be snubbed and excluded from the Caucasian Children's World. I expected "them" to be my enemies. Since then, I have found that you cannot judge a person or persons by their color or your first instinct but by their personality.

Ninety per cent of my friends are Negro. Not because I want it that way, but because I was brought up with the facts of racial barriers.

I am still shy about white friends, as most of the Negroes at Garfield are, but I am still pushing ahead—first out of my shell and into integration. With my hand in a Caucasian girl's hand, we shall pull though the "Jim Crow Chains," link by link.

"Caesura" has been most illuminating. In 1964-1965, that first year of integrated Garfield, the magazine was dominated by interracial concern and introspection. The next year, in the June, 1967, issue, Marsha, whose essay I just quoted, wrote a poem called "Hope."

Hope, black man, Hope.
But don't stop digging.
    For your dreams and hopes
will never untangle the vines.

Many of the Garfield and West Campus boys and girls, white and black, went on "digging" into their differences and similarities at retreats sponsored at nearby camps by the Berkeley office of the federal Elementary and Secondary Education Act. They dug beneath the tangled vines, got at some of the roots of prejudice as they talked, danced, swam, and played. One 13-year-old Garfield girl wrote down her reactions when she got home from one of these outings:

I went on the retreat to have fun, meet people, and try to get to feel more comfortable with Negroes, although I didn't feel very hopeful of the latter. I knew before I went that in the discussions nothing much would be established in terms of my own peace of mind and the relationships between all of the people. I was right about the discussion groups; wrong about the Negroes.

The Negro boys always looked the same to me before, and they never seemed particularly interesting. On the retreat they began to stand out as individuals. Traits that I had always noticed on white boys began to appear to me on the Negro boys. Some were handsome, some were immature. Some were friendly and some were poor sports. Others were fun to be with. I'm not saying that they are the same as the white boys, because they're not. They have a uniqueness all their own. They have something the whites don't have; the whites have something they don't have. I have found that they are equally fun to be with, once I get accepted which is sometimes hard cause I am white and they are black. On the retreat, my friend and I sat at a table at lunch that had all Negro boys, except for one white boy. We were the only girls and it was fun because the whole table really had spirit.

I don't feel differently toward the Negro girls. I never felt uncomfortable in their presence, but I never felt like they were the same as me in any way. I am not saying that I can't have a friend unless they're similar to me; I have Negro friends. I am not satisfied with my relationships with Negro girls. Something important is missing that I can't pinpoint yet.

Unlike Garfield, West Campus moved naturally toward true integration, after desegregation. But that does not mean that the students did not work at it.

A very successful retreat of West Campus students helped to bring home to them how much many of them had in common. Seventy-four West Campus students—46 girls, 28 boys—almost equally black and white in numbers, went up the coast to camp with teachers, YMCA staff members, and professionals in psychology and social planning. They had two days—two days of heavy rain—to talk, to sing, to dance.

"Nothing mattered," wrote one of the adults there, "except what a person was like inside. The real problems turned out to be common problems. That is what they discovered and this is what bound them together. Common problems of living—such as getting along, learning to dance, achieving in school, being liked, making friends."

Music—disagreement over the kind of records played at dances—was found to be a dividing force symbolizing a deeper separation. Why don't Negro kids like Beatle records? Why don't white kids like soul music written by Negroes? A Negro student said, "Maybe you're afraid we can dance better than you," and a white student admitted, "I don't know how to dance the way you do." By the end of the retreat, little clusters of students were teaching each other their different ways of dancing.

"That's the answer," said one. "You help us and we'll help you."

Such seemingly surface common problems led into deep and therapeutic exploration of basic differences. "We" and "they" were repeated over and over. "What is a Negro person? He is one who feels 'outside' and tries to act superior as a defense. He acts a 'better-than-you-are' role because he doesn't feel 'in.'" . . . "White people act superior but underneath they feel guilty and afraid because they know, deep inside, what justice and morality mean." . . . "People fight to hide their true feelings. . . . It would do us all a lot of good to admit our faults.". . . "If people have something to do together, they can grow to understand each other. If they stay separate, they never will."

The students came back to school with the following suggestions for change:

• Increase the size of the Student Relations Council.
• Conduct a day-long, school-wide discussion on race relations.
• Change the tracking system.
• Repair, somehow, some of the attitudes some teachers have toward minority peoples.
• Integrate the elementary schools.
• Establish seminars and courses of study on Negro history and culture and on race relations.
• Make more intergroup living experiences available to more students.
• Conduct music assemblies.
• Bring the subject of prejudice more out into the open.

The students returned determined to maintain the interracial friendships they had made. They said that if others sneered at these friendships, "then they're not worth having as friends."

We adults, administrators and teachers, were also constantly learning and growing. We soon recognized areas of school life that if changed could help the whole process of integration. I have insisted since the Ramsey Plan began that emphasis be placed on sports, music and art and drama—the areas which all children love and in which many Negroes excel. I have insisted that the lunch break be arranged for the maximum mixing of races. All this has helped. Improvement is evidenced in every area. We have done much more than simply to redistrict, much more than just feeding Negro and white bodies into the same school.

Had we predicted what type of changes in student performance would take place *first* in desegregation, we would probably have said social changes rather than academic. And, as I say again and again, social change is implicit as we work toward integration—social change is a part of education. One of our seventh-grade counselors compared citizenship marks of seventh-grade children who attended the segregated Burbank Junior High School with those of seventh-grade ghetto children who are now attending the desegregated Garfield. (Citizenship tests checking responsible attitudes toward the student body and larger community are marked subjectively by teachers.) She has found that ghetto children have a significantly better chance to obtain satisfactory citizenship marks in the integrated Garfield situation than they would have had if they had attended the "old Burbank." The number of poor citizenship marks was reduced by about 50 per cent.

Garfield's principal attributes this improvement to

• Community concern and acceptance involving minority races as reflected on the campus.

• A greater number of academically-oriented "models" for the less academically-oriented student.

• Willingness of minority students to identify with teachers in the integrated situation.

• Teacher realization of problems of the disadvantaged.

I must disagree with the last reason, however. "Teacher realization of problems of the disadvantaged" was not general. It was very hard for many of the Garfield teachers, long accustomed to high-achieving, all-white students, to adjust to the new black and white mixture. Some could change, some couldn't. I must also point out that teacher integration, with more Negro teachers brought into Garfield, was not moving ahead. As Dr. Thomas Wogaman, my special assistant, expressed it: "Ghandi himself could have learned some passive resistance techniques from some of the 'old-school' teachers."

Berkeley hired its first Negro teachers—only two—in 1950. They were placed in kindergarten due to the stereotype that Negroes are used to caring for little children. Even then these two pioneers, highly trained and experienced, were watched by parents who stood back of the playground fence. As the first Negro kindergarten teachers "proved safe," they were allowed to advance into grades and subject areas in which they had been trained. By the time secondary integration began in 1964 Berkeley had a comparatively large proportion of Negro teachers, two Negro principals, and a number of Negroes in administrative positions. The district was actively recruiting more. Garfield, due to its tight "prestige" position, was one of a very few—I'd say two or three—schools in the whole district where teacher integration had not been achieved.

At West Campus, the newly integrated all-ninth grade plant that had been the almost totally Negro Burbank Junior High School, Negro and white teachers had worked together for a long time. This made a great difference. Adjustment to an interrracial student body was much less difficult. Also the principal had administered old Burbank for many years, whereas Garfield's principal had come to Berkeley only two years before desegregation began and had become principal at the same time the Ramsey Plan was implemented.

In other ways too West Campus had built-in factors to make it succeed in integrating. A comparison of West Campus with Garfield would be unfair. Parents had not strongly opposed the change and the students were hepped up about having their own school of just ninth-graders. "An air of expectancy runs through everything. Students expect much of themselves. Teachers have high expectations for them," the principal reports. The school seemed right. "It's a brighter age here now. And the reason is that West Campus is now for all students, no matter where they live in the city."

Old bitter feelings were washed away. "The students did have feelings about Burbank being for just one group of people. The parents had feelings about it too. Everybody's level of self-esteem has been raised, now that the school serves the whole community, not just one part of it. . . . Our boys and girls are doing fine in the new system. They have a sense of social justice. They know what's right."

"And the community around the school has changed in its attitude because of the change at West Campus. The people of the neighborhood feel more a part of the whole city because they see students from throughout the city coming into their area daily. . . . The change at school has given the community around it a feeling of belonging to one town rather than an isolated region within it."

We still have a long way to go before we can call our Ramsey Plan schools—the two junior high schools and West Campus—truly integrated. Berkeley High School, desegregated long ago by the accident of being the one and only high school, certainly cannot be called integrated. But it grows better year by year as the students come in from desegregated West Campus by way of the desegregated junior high schools.

West Campus, as its principal said, is the most hopeful. But Garfield is making the breakthrough. Racial barriers are going down. At the end of the Ramsey Plan's third year (1967) the Garfield girls' track team, an almost 50-50 mixture of Negroes and whites, went to Oakland to compete with the girls' track team at an almost totally Negro school. When the Oakland team saw Garfield's black and white team, they berated and sneered at the Berkeley Negroes. Garfield's Negro girls stood their ground. Backed by their white teammates, they shouted back at their Negro opposition: "What's the matter with you anyway? You don't live in the world! You don't know what's going on! You're a bunch of squares!"

Garfield won the track meet. Garfield will struggle through.

9

The Buses Begin to Roll

"WHAT DO YOU WANT FOR YOUR CHILDREN?"
That was the searching question posed to Berkeley parents by the Board of Education on November 16, 1965, and during the three months that followed. That is the question parents are facing, or should be facing all over the United States.

During this, the second year of secondary school integration, we proposed to take what the community would certainly consider a "giant step"—busing a few young children to schools out of their neighborhoods. In the spring of 1964, when the Ramsey Plan was approved, the board had tabled "indefinitely" a sweeping elementary redistricting by busing which had been recommended by a school staff task force. Now, in fall 1965, only a year and a half later, we were recommending the use of federal funds, newly provided by the Elementary and Secondary Education Act, Title I, to bus 238 Negro children from the four overcrowded elementary schools in south and west Berkeley to the middle and hill schools. There was room in these "receiving schools" for that number, and transferring would reduce class size in ghetto schools to 28. We hoped to begin the program in February, 1966, some three months later, after intensive public discussion. The school district had applied for a grant of $513,000, under the new ESEA, to be used over a three year period, to improve the educational opportunities in the four schools of south and west Berkeley and funds for busing some children out of the schools was included in the request. Our application, we were told, was near the top of the pile. Reduced class size was the A-1 need.

The 238 children were to be selected as those who could most easily make the transition. We would not be deliberately selecting high achievers, although some of course would be among them. Our selection, made by teachers and principals, would be a cross-section, based on those who were getting along well in school—children who had no record of truancy or trouble-making, who had adjusted well to their home schools and who therefore could be expected to adjust well to the new situation.

The ESEA mandate required that the half-million be spent on "the special educational needs of children of low-income families and the impact that concentrations of low-income families has on the ability of local educational agencies to support adequate educational programs." Those needs in Berkeley were concentrated in the four-school area stretching north to south across lower Berkeley where most of the population is Negro. Our three-year plan for use of the funds included smaller classes in the project area; improvement of reading, speaking, and writing skills; helping teachers to teach better; helping parents to help their children learn; more and better equipment and materials; more personnel; and the busing program which would use up only approximately $37,000 per year.

This would be voluntary busing in that no child would be bused without parents' consent and by signed agreement. But it would be administered by the school district, not a parent-run program like those in many cities which almost seem planned to fail. It would not be subject to parents' change of mind nor to a child's failure to adjust except in extreme cases. Once a child was launched by bus into the new school, he would stay there through his elementary life.

The bus ride to and from school would take only 15 to 20 minutes per child per day, and the distance covered would be only one and a half to two miles. The cost would be only $86.72 per child per year or 48 cents per day per child. This, we construed, could be paid by ESEA-Title I funds allotted for the improvement of poverty ("target") area schools, where one of the major needs was reduced class size. Our interpretation of the intent of the federal law was unique, but we made our case, although state authorities who administered the federal funds were somewhat reluctant. However, the state would not allow us to use ESEA funds for the 11 and one half extra teachers needed to accommodate the 238 pupils transferred to middle Berkeley and hill schools. The district had to pay that expense.

"What do you want for your children?" was suddenly of immediate concern to Berkeley parents. Would the majority of the Negro parents give the answer—"Quality, integrated education?" The burden of the plan lay on them. Their children would be taken out of their familiar surroundings, out of neighborhood schools. Would they understand the need and make the sacrifice? In many cities Negro parents had hesitated and refused to take this step. In Berkeley, we felt, due to their support of the schools in general and of secondary integration in particular, that we could count on them now.

We could make no such assumptions about the Caucasian parents. *Their* children were receiving quality education already, if one understands quality to mean high academic standards only. Would they understand that monoracial education, in the all-white setting, is neither complete nor quality education in an interracial nation? Would some assume that with the "target" (poverty area) schools enriched by these new federal funds, the 238 Negro children could get quality education by staying in the ghetto?

The plan came before the school board two weeks after the public announcement on November 16, 1965. The board meeting was attended by a cross-section of parents from all over the city. It had been widely publicized in a San Francisco newspaper, widely read in Berkeley, that jumped the gun by saying in a page one headline, "Berkeley Will Bus Negro Children." This came as a surprise since the plan had not yet been officially presented nor approved by the board.

Nothing was being sprung on the public, however. Nothing was being sprung (or ever could be) on the board. But the board had not yet *acted*, nor was it going to act for two more weeks. Ever since the previous May, over six months, discussion had been pursued intensively by board members, school administration, teaching staff, PTA's, League of Women Voters, Chamber of Commerce, church groups. Plans were made, criticized, revised and studied again. Hundreds of teachers, including both teachers' organizations, had been involved. Administrators brought the plan into every speech they were asked to make. I never missed a chance to discuss it, whether I had been asked to speak on reading, New Math, or high potential children.

Although the administration carried the responsibility of coordinating the discussions, of consolidating the ideas, and of actually developing the formal proposal to the board, the ESEA proposal adopted by the board, in a real sense, can be claimed by hundreds of school staff members and lay citizens as theirs. I doubt that the degree of participation by the community and school staff in developing this program will be matched by any comparable city in the United States.

The press story of the plan as a fait accompli caused a hullabaloo. I was working at home and reporters, unable to get my unlisted phone number, drove up to my house to question me. All I could answer was, "Well, it isn't true yet, but I'm darned sure it's going to be if Board of Education leadership means what I think it does to this community."

The news lead served us well. It brought out the crowd; it brought out hot arguments pro and con. It was an exciting and healthy board meeting, lasting five and a half hours.

"Let's look at it for what it is," board member John Miller had urged. "It's a means of helping disadvantaged children by lowering class size. There's room in the east— the middle and hill schools—and not in the south and west project schools."

This small pilot venture could be a major step toward total elementary integration. I construed the intention of the ESEA to mean that we were to do whatever we could to improve education in the project area, predominantly Negro schools, and if busing some of them out of the ghetto to reduce class size was one way, ESEA would pay for it. Further, I said, if we do not reduce class size we may not get the grant. I went out on a limb with that statement, but I believed it, although I was one of only a few superintendents—if not the only one—who thus interpreted the grant. And as one small lever to gain consensus, that argument worked. No community, least of all Berkeley, wants to lose its chance for half a million dollars in school aid.

But busing was a bad word in Berkeley. The Ramsey Plan for secondary school children, ages 12 and up, was implemented. It contained no busing. And in the spring of 1964 the board had tabled "indefinitely" the proposed elementary redistricting plan which did mean busing. Now it was November, 1965. The ESEA program planned to begin in February, 1966, was certainly *not* elementary redistricting. Only a few Negro children and no white children were being bused; and it could hardly be called major desegregation when only 238 children out of our Negro elementary population of 3,573 were involved. The board was not breaking its pledge.

Was it busing that Berkeley parents feared? Or was the bus now, as in May, 1964, the symbol of opposition to integration? What was so earth-shaking about this move? Parents, admittedly very few, in many cities—in Boston, Chicago, and even in conservative Orange County, California—have bused their children (paying for it themselves) in the interests of integration. More than 2,000 Berkeley children—approximately one-ninth of its total school population—attend private schools, one-third of them in other cities; and at least 25 take the bus daily to San Francisco and another 20 to Marin County, 20 miles away. Compare that to our maximum *two* miles of transportation. No, parents did not really fear or oppose transporting young children to school. Most of the Negro parents, however, had to face sending their children into a strange world. Some of the white parents feared busing would bring a disturbing experience for their children—a breaking into their snug white world by these strangers. Busing of Negro children also implied the threat that their children might one day be bused out of *their* security.

Who were the fearful? Who were the brave? Who were the secure and unafraid? All had the opportunity to express themselves fully, in fear or in confidence, at meetings, held for combined school populations in representative parts of the city, following that board presentation of the plan on November 16, 1965.

Let me report one such meeting held by Hillside and Cragmont, two prestigious schools in the most beautiful and economically privileged hill area of Berkeley. This one lasted until 2 a.m. and steamed with argument and invective. When I walked into that meeting at 7:45 p.m., I sensed the hostility. I recognized some of the citizens who had so aggressively opposed the Ramsey Plan, some upper middle-class persons who had supported a hill candidate for board member who ran on a "keep the neighborhood school" plank (and was defeated), and a number of Negroes whom I identified as both for and against us. I also saw some of the Old Berkeley group who always hold out against change. I saw some of the fanatic and frantic fringe. And I was sure many of the people there had no children in the schools, probably never had had, but were there to protect their all-white schools in the midst of all-white property.

I was reassured only by friendly clusters of white and Negro parents talking warmly together. These were the parents who had led mixed groups of Girl Scouts, Boy Scouts, and Campfire Girls and who had been active in the hills-flats "Sister School" program. How great was their strength?

The speakers ranged from true activist liberals to hard-core racists, from courageous Negro leaders to Uncle Toms. Some of the Uncle Tom type, whom Old Berkeley likes so well, had been briefed on what to say by white reactionaries. The polished, sophisticated hill Caucasians, of course, would not be caught dead voicing obvious prejudice or bigotry—they expressed it in roundabout ways. "Compassion" was one way. In the words of one, "It will be too hard for the Negro children to leave their homes and neighborhoods. They'll be lonely up here."

Quietly, one Negro mother responded: "Yes, we know, they will be lonely at first. They've been lonely before. Some of us have been lonely all our lives!"

Old Berkeleyans held forth on the old "don't rock the boat" theme. "Let's help the Negroes where they are. Let's spend the money on them down there. We've always been good to our Negroes here in Berkeley. We've always got along all right with them. They're happy *where they are!*"

Plenty of Negro listeners flinched at this kind of statement.

The whites did not hide their fear that the achievement of their children, many of them gifted, would be downgraded or diluted by what they considered—and what *was*, on the average—the lower academic standard of the Negro pupils. Speakers countered with reports of research showing that desegregation does not lower the achievement of white children while it raises the achievement level of Negro children. "Oh, research!" one white parent muttered. "You can prove anything with research."

Then one Negro mother (it seems the Negro mothers were doing most of the talking that night) stood up. "I see what it is—you're afraid of Negro kids!" she declared. "Why? We have something to offer you but you've always turned us down. What if *our* children should slip back in their studies by coming up here? Did you ever think of that?"

That statement got loud applause from many Negroes and from some startled Caucasians. Could it be that Negroes *too* worried about scholarship? The ironic nature of that meeting would have been funny had it not been so painful.

"To wait"—"to wait until. . . ." that was what many white parents as well as many Negro parents wanted. To wait another generation. . . . to let "my" child stay put where he is. . . . not to use one's child to further one's belief in integration. To accomplish it gradually, as one white parent put it, improving the ghetto schools (certainly by federal money), waiting until *they*, the Negro children, caught up with *us*, the whites, and then "integration will come."

One Negro mother, after such a white gradualist spoke, answered: "What do you mean—it'll come? By magic? There ain't gonna be no magic! We've gotta do it ourselves."

Standing up and turning to face the audience, another Negro mother looked into the white faces and said: "We've been waiting ever since the Civil War. We can't wait any longer!"

Well, we just squeaked through with consensus at that Hillside-Cragmont meeting. The proposal had an equally hard time at the meeting at Thousand Oaks School, centered in an area composed partly of upper- and middle-class homeowners and partly of working-class small homeowners. The former were mainly stand-pat conservatives; the latter felt any move for racial equality threatened to diminish the property value of their homes. Here had been the hardcore resistance to Berkeley's fair housing ordinance and later to the Ramsey integration plan. Here they were less polite. They said what they thought: "Don't bring Negroes here!" But here, too, were liberal leaders who supported our proposal.

Starkly contrasting to these superficial and really self-centered concerns expressed in meetings in white schools were the problems of Negro parents in the ghetto schools who must decide whether or not to bus their children. At Columbus School, the principal headed directly into the heart of the matter with the question: "What are some of the things you want for your children?" "To be happy". . . . "To learn to get along with other kinds of people". . . . "To have a better life than we have had". . . ."To learn how to live in the world the way it is". . . . "To be able to get a better job than we ever could."

The first answer stirred a discussion on the nature and value of happiness. "But my child is happy *here*, he's doing well in school, he loves his teacher," several parents said.

The principal's answer was logical but a hard concept to assimilate. "If your child has been happy here, he will be able to be happy there," he said. "If he's been getting along well here, he will get along well there. It's *because* he's been happy here that he's been chosen to be transferred."

Truly a hard one to grasp—because your child has been happy here, we're sending him away. The burden was on the Negro child. He might be afraid, he could be lonely, he could function below the white children in his studies and therefore be ashamed and diminished. And the burden was on the child's parents, who must decide whether to separate him from his neighborhood, his friends and sisters and brothers, or to keep him safe here in the ghetto.

"What is happiness?" asked a Negro mother of two who was a school counselor. She came from the rural South, made her way through the educational mill there and in the north, gained self-assurance, strength, and leadership. Happiness had not always been her lot. She had spent weeks going from door to door explaining the busing proposal. "Your child will be away from you a bit," she said. "Perhaps he *will* be a little less happy for a while. But think of his future: Will he be happier in a world that is our Negro world, with all the handicaps we Negroes know, or in a world of Negro and white together as it is meant to be and can become?"

The hard thing was that this was "for keeps"—the child going to the new school now would stay through the sixth grade. Of course it had to be that way. One could feel the pain in the parents' hearts. "Why can't we wait till they're bigger?" some asked. "Why move them now? When they're bigger, they can take it better." "My child's scared to go." . . . and "My little girl cries when she thinks about it and although I want her to go I don't know if I should let her."

"Are you scared to have them go?" "Do they know

you're scared, even when you say you want them to go? If you're scared, they know it, and it makes them afraid. If *you're* not, *they'll* be all right."

To many working parents, who had to leave home early and arrange for their children to walk to the bus or ride with other friends, the new schedule—the new and unaccustomed plan—would present a hardship. They discussed this. Some were newcomers from the rural South, still timid in the new city and as yet without friends. Other parents spoke up and offered to pick their children up and take them to the bus for them or to send their older children to escort them to the bus stop.

On the other hand, there were many parents who expressed their pride that their children had been selected. A few commented that their children have friends in the hills —perhaps in Boy Scout or Girl Scout troops or Campfire Girls—and would be happy now to be able to see them every day.

Several Negro parents pointed out that their children were in the "fast group" in their present school—would they be able to do as well in the new one? The answer: Compatible grouping would prevail.

There was a sophisticated joke among some Negro parents who were committed to the busing move. "I'm having to fight the bigotry in this Negro neighborhood."

All these feelings were aired. Everybody obviously felt free to speak. A striking thing was the fact that no hostility was expressed by the Negroes toward white children or white schools. Another outstanding thing was their pride in race: they wanted their children to be good representatives. They said this in several ways: "I know my boy will behave just fine, the way he does here," or "White kids are good and bad, just like ours are."

All doubts, all fears were expressed. But the value of integration, even with those who wished the process could be postponed, *was* understood and accepted. Almost nobody, however, felt the process would be easy. The first hard task, for schools and parents, was to tell, persuade, and prepare the children. Principals discussed ways and means together, then chose the ways they thought best for their school population. Parents also met together and then tackled the job in the way they felt was best.

Some parents told their children they were changing schools so they could get to know other children. Others said it was because the schools were smaller. Others told their children that integration was the reason—that they were warriors in the cause of equality. Most parents reported they did not dwell on the reasons. Some were deliberately very casual, saying such things as: "It's new and worth a try." "It's good to do different things." "The bus ride will be fun." "Change is an adventure." The parents reported that they tried not to make the situation too serious. They did not want their children to expect friction.

Not a day or evening passed without a meeting—PTA meetings in Negro and white schools, joint Negro and white meetings, inter-school meetings, workshops for teachers. Our Intergroup Education Project worked manfully at its task. It held 150 group meetings in the schools, providing speakers and literature about the values of integration, the pain and damage caused by discrimination and segregation, the contributions of Negroes—cultural and historic—and the weakness of the monoracial school in the Negro or white ghetto.

Meanwhile the schools in middle Berkeley and the hills that were to receive the new students prepared parents and children. Cragmont planned a "big-brother, big-sister" pairing program for the incoming children; Thousand Oaks parents planned a person-to-person "buddy" system with Franklin Negro parents. The principal of Whittier school in middle Berkeley, where there was already a cross-section, including a few Negro children, children of young UC students, and children in lower-income brackets, felt it best not to emphasize the change. "I believe there is the danger of overdramatizing and overemphasizing what is essentially only the addition of a few children to the Whittier student body," he said. He planned to make the newcomers feel a part of Whittier's student body as quickly as possible through his own and his teachers' efforts. But he felt that more than casual discussion of the change with children would only make them self-conscious and accentuate the "differentness."

Hillside school, however, was a different situation—an old, heretofore impregnable, prestige school needing intensive preparation. The principal suggested that parents discuss together anticipated problems at a joint PTA meeting of the hill and ghetto schools. He was concerned to open up communication between the schools before busing began so that understanding of actual problems after February, 1966, would be enhanced. He wanted to bring out in the open the fears of both groups about the academic standards of the school, aggression, and respect for personal property. He asked the parents to discuss the deeply personal questions, what do parents from Columbus, Whittier, and Hillside agree upon as being important values for their families and for their children.

I think the principal was right in bringing up these questions. "Can those Columbus children read in kindergarten?" asked the parent of a precocious child at one of these meetings. She was answered, however, by another parent who said: "What's so sacrosanct about reading in kindergarten?"

And another parent said: "Well, our children aren't hostile but they think the Negro children will be hostile."

And there was one parent who said, tight-lipped and grimly: "Well, we have done other things we didn't want to do and we can do this."

Within the school, the principal set up a four-week orientation program to develop more positive attitudes. In all classes the program adapted to age-level was this: the first week the children discussed with the teacher "Common needs of all children—food, shelter, acceptance by others"; the second week, "What it's like to be new in a school"; the third week, "Learning how to make new-comers feel welcome" (this was the week of an open house for the newcomers with "host and hostess" committees); and the fourth week, just before the busing, they got ready for the newcomers—moved desks, prepared name tags, selected books, and shared in other chores. Some sophisticated parents thought this program was "Sunday-school-ish," but obviously the children relished it. And it worked.

Now the PTA's of the receiving schools sent letters of welcome to the parents of the incoming children. All held receptions for the parents and children. Hillside's reception was significant. One saw a number of cars drive up—Negro and white parents, Negro and white children together. In some cases the white parents had picked up the Negro family; in some cases the Negro family picked up its white counterpart. There were also Hillside parents who came in stiffly and stood apart. One white mother came into the Negro midst groaning audibly, and her child clung tightly to her hand.

The Negro parents came also in toto, and some found it easy to be sociable. A few were shy; some had been re-luctant to come. One mother said, "Well, I'll send my girl up there but I'm not going up there!" The counselor immediately responded. "Now, I don't want to hear any more remarks like that. You *go* up there!" And that mother, as well as the rest, *did* go.

As for the children, they just enjoyed themselves. All the Negro children were invited to their receiving school once, sometimes twice, to get acquainted, play on the playground, enjoy refreshments. The appointed young hosts and hostesses did their job well. Everybody had fun. Then there were tryout bus rides, and of course the kids loved those.

As February 1, the day busing would begin, approached, it looked as if our carefully prepared integration step—small, but achieved against typical fears—was going to work. If there was anything we hadn't done in preparation, I can't think what it was.

The parents were ready. The teachers were ready. The children were ready—more truly ready than we knew.

10

The Buses Reach
Their Destination

ON FEBRUARY 1, 1966, came the first bus ride to the schools in middle Berkeley and the hills to which 238 Negro children had been assigned for the rest of their elementary years—the first day of classes, the first mixing on the playground. How would it work; how would it feel?

At Hillside School, the children had discussed how the new children would feel when they came to Hillside. They recognized the fear and loneliness they themselves would feel if they had to change schools. "They probably are going to be scared". . . . "I would be very scared and shy". . . . "I would feel scared that someone is going to make a joke about me". . . . "We might fight with them, we might tease them, but they might do the same to us". . . . "I would feel mad and quite frightened". . . . "When I came here from Houston, Texas, I was good and scared, and these new kids will feel the same way". . . . "New kids feel scared of everybody. They're afraid to do anything wrong because they think everybody will laugh". . . . "You feel funny about everything at first. Everyone looks like strangers. You don't know anyone so you play by yourself."

The Hillside pupils had made suggestions in class, such as: "I feel if we all try to make friends with them they will not feel so shy and unwanted". . . . "We should try to get along and be good friends with them". . . . "We can show them around the school". . . . "I am going to help these kids feel comfortable here, sort of like they were still at Columbus."

And a very practical idea: "When the new kids come, I will tell them where the bathroom is."

From the Administration Building we followed the whole move carefully. Evelyn Stewart, in her "public information specialist" role, turned reporter and watched it personally during those first busing days and at intervals thereafter, looking and listening, talking with children, teachers, counselors, bus drivers, and custodians. I shall long remember her return from the first day of the busing project as she came into an administrative staff meeting to report her enthusiasm. That first day she rode the bus with the Negro group from Lincoln School in the ghetto to their new base at Emerson in the hills, and her report reflects the excitement.

The Lincoln children, kindergarteners to mid-sixth-graders, mounted the bus at 8:15 a.m. at the designated pickup point—a sidestreet leading into a main thoroughfare that runs from ghetto to hills. A Negro mother, employed as an aide for the first few weeks, was there with them. So was one of the neighborhood aides employed to supervise the whole bus-riding operation as it got started. A few mothers had come to see their children off. There was the big yellow bus and its driver, a lean Texan in blue jeans and jacket and big black cowboy hat. "Hi, kids!" he said, then corrected himself and said, "Good morning, girls and boys!" "Hi!" they responded, and, then, copying him, "Good morning!" Pretty soon, as they waited to mount the bus, one child got up the courage to ask him, "Are you a cowboy?" and the driver answered, "Sure enough. I used to be." Now the kids felt better.

It was a cool grey morning—what Berkeley calls cool at 65 degrees—with rain possible, although just as likely the sun would emerge about 10 o'clock and shine brightly.

Some of the boys wore shiny black or yellow slickers and fireman's rainhats. Every child was well dressed, most of them in simple neat school clothes, a few—at their request —in their Sunday best because this was a big day in their lives. Almost every reporter who covered the first busing day remarked on how well the children were dressed, how neatly groomed, writing as if the white race has a monopoly on pride in good appearance.

Although the children had ridden the bus before on a "dry run"—a get-acquainted ride, including a visit to their "new" school—the experience was still new and fresh. The children clustered together, sitting close to one another, some chattering and giggling as the bus rode upward, some quiet—slowly at first through early morning traffic, more rapidly as it mounted into the hills. They saw University student apartments, with pairs of socks or shirts hanging to dry in the window, an assortment of gift shops, art galleries, coffee houses, street cafes, churches quite unlike the simple ones they attended, the cluster of modern dormitories termed the "UC Hiltons," students hurrying to the University on foot, bicycles and Hondas—all comprising a different glimpse of living from what they knew. As they drove up into the residential section, they saw big old houses painted much less recently than their own, also many fine new ones. They saw beautiful gardens. But how much they took in on this exciting first day is a question.

The older children sat in pairs or small groups. Some sat alone. One sixth-grade boy who sat apart, looking tense and serious, was asked if he was glad to be going to Emerson. "At first I wasn't, but now I am," he said. "I liked it at Lincoln with my friends. But after I talked a lot with my teachers and parents, I decided I wanted to go. Anyway, I decided I ought to go."

Soon they arrived at Emerson—all too short a ride for the little ones who love to ride buses, and for the older ones who were more aware of their burden as ghetto pioneers entering a new world. Now they had to leave the security of the bus and the friendly cowboy driver and enter the strange white school. The Emerson children were waiting for them on the playground. The principal, a grave man of few but well-chosen words, was standing at the bright red door of the newly modernized school and almost before the bus came to a stop he walked out to welcome them. He stepped into the bus. "Good morning, boys and girls," he said. "Welcome to your new school. Your teachers are ready, your classrooms are ready. Are *you* ready?"

The children answered with one loud and hearty, "Yes!"

They entered the playground gate slowly in a single file. In no time at all, however, girls and boys in red caps, who had been assigned or had volunteered as hosts and guides, came to them, said "Hi," and began mingling them with the others to go into the classrooms. Some stood apart smiling self-consciously. Once in the classrooms, it was "business as usual," no palaver—just the first day of the spring semester when all must be briefed on such routine matters as what to do with lunch money and the usual regulations.

On the second day, Mrs. Stewart rode the bus to Hillside School with the children from Columbus. This was an even more dramatic ride—a more striking glimpse of how the other half lives, for the approach to Hillside winds steeply upward on a narrow road through some of the most beautiful homes in Berkeley. Hillside is an old grey stone building, its arched entrance a great carved oaken door that might be the entrance to a church. Although the surroundings are wooded and the houses with their fine gardens merge in friendly fashion into the school grounds, it must have seemed awesome to the new children.

Carefully prepared by their principal the young hosts

and hostesses were busy making the new children feel at home. One Hillside boy was heard saying to a new boy, "Hey, I'm your buddy, you know. You gotta play with me."

In the days that followed we gathered many more significant glimpses and heard of many interesting incidents at the hill schools. White children seemed to use mainly language to get acquainted; Negro children tended to use the sense of touch. With boys, whatever their color, the sense of touch often meant friendly wrestling and often, too, not so friendly fighting. Boys at certain age levels just have to express themselves with their bodies, tumbling and rolling around together.

Two Negro boys were seen slugging a white boy. Standing nearby was a white sixth-grader—a quiet, intellectual boy. He moved up and said: "That is no way to solve your problems." His quiet criticism was so startling that the boys immediately stopped their punching and walked away.

The girls had playground problems, too. It turned out that the Negro girls jumped rope faster, higher, and longer than the white girls could. When the best Negro jumper of all was excluded from the game, a noisy argument ensued which ended in the vice-principal's office. The vice-principal took them to task, rather in the manner of a coach. "We play fair," he said, "or we don't play." He discussed the problems of getting acquainted, of learning to work and play together, and wound up philosophically with the comment, "Some people are better in some things; some, in others. That's the way life is."

Some of the problems were more serious than playground tussles. Many newcomers needed individual attention. A fourth-grade teacher at Cragmont found herself using a little spontaneous therapy on Henry, a Negro newcomer. Henry is a little boy, almost the smallest in the class. He had a history of problems but had been regarded as sufficiently stable to be transferred. Also he had begged to go because his older sister would be enrolled in an upper class. But in the new classroom, Henry was aggressively hostile, easily upset, a troublemaker. He talked back to his teacher and pushed younger children around on the playground. One day, his teacher reported, he came in and she saw that the whole class, including some Negro classmates, had turned against him.

"He was so alone," his teacher said. "I felt sorry for him. I just went to him and wrapped my arms around him tight, then led him to his desk. The other children looked sort of surprised but also pleased. This helped Henry, but I don't know if it will last."

Meanwhile his sister—a beautiful girl, self-confident and a good mixer—was a shining star in the sixth-grade. Within a few weeks her class elected her group captain. Another Negro girl stood out at once for her ability in creative writing and music composition. She wrote for the school magazine and composed a song for her class.

The few children of upper middle-class Negro families who have long lived in the hill area reacted variously according to their personalities. One, who is lively, attractive and popular in her hill school—a "big wheel"—mixed spontaneously with the less privileged newcomers. The new Negro girls were proud of her and she became for some a model; they too tried to be outgoing, lively and popular. Another hill Negro student was torn and miserable when the "outside" Negro children came into the school. She was sorry for the new girls. "They're lonely and unhappy," she said, when asked how the girls were getting along. "They want to go home," she said. But she herself could not help them. She stayed apart from the newcomers, clung to her long-time white chum.

The younger the children were, the easier the adjustment was. But not for all. David, a second-grader, was one of several who begged to go back to his old school. He was an appealing little fellow, who almost never smiled. He missed his friends and his sisters and brothers downtown. "No, I *don't* like it," he insisted. "They don't play with you. The bus is the only part I like. I wish I could never get off!"

David's parents also asked if he could be returned to his former school, but had to be told, despite understanding and sympathy for the child, that he could not. Implicit in the agreement of transfer—and necessarily so—was that it would last long enough to be given a fair chance.

Some interesting generalizations emerged. With the exception of young David and a few others his age, primary-grade children mixed easily. They were interested in external differences like skin and hair but basically they felt alike and quickly became good friends. They played happily together, shared notes on scrapes and bruises, exchanged toys, learned to accept one another. Here as one counselor expressed it are "school kid" personality problems, not white kid or black kid problems.

It was much harder for fifth- and sixth-graders. Some as a group, others separately, set themselves apart. At Whittier, some of the transfer students formed a sports team and would not let anyone else in. They would not even play with the other Negroes from the Whittier area. They apparently came to Whittier feeling different and insisted on reinforcing that feeling. The principal and teachers broke up the clique by talking it over and by relentlessly insisting that they include other players. "But the change is on the surface," said one deeply concerned teacher. "The boys have been guided into mixing with their fellows. But in their hearts, they still feel separate and apart. Perhaps, for them—at ages 11 and 12—integration is too late."

The older Negro girls, by and large, adjusted better

than the boys, both socially and academically. A few fifth-
and sixth-grade boys, when they could not keep pace with
their white contemporaries in the classroom turned sullen
and recalcitrant. Back and forth they went to the principal's office. Some got over the hurdle, some did not. This,
however, is the usual boy-girl growth difference—the girls
mature earlier, more quickly gain social skills. If the Negro
girls were lonely and afraid, they concealed it in the classroom. But in the nurse's room, unoccupied when the part-
time nurse was not there, one often found a Negro girl,
excused from the classroom for "not feeling well," lying on
the couch to rest a while. And soon a friend "from home"
came to sit with her.

As the busing transfer progressed, a graduate student
in education at San Francisco State College, and a Berkeley
parent, made a study of feelings of social belonging at
Emerson School. She chose Emerson because, although its
school population is primarily Caucasian, its children
come from diverse backgrounds—from families of University faculty, business and professional fields and single-
parent homes—and the area is primarily middle income.

Her sample totaled 107 children of whom 19, or 18 per
cent, were Negro transfers from Lincoln School. The children queried were in grades 3, 4, 5, and 6. They were
asked to state in order their choice of three people in the
class they would like to sit by. Some were then interviewed
about their choice or rejection. Interviews went like this:
Q. "On the card you put some choices of those you would
like to sit by in school. How did you happen to choose her
(or him)?" The children's typical answers were either general statements, He's my best friend. I like him; or expressed a special relationship; We play together. She helps
me. He gives me things; or revealed attributes and behavior they admired. She's pretty. The other kids like her.
She's a good student. Or, in case of rejection, opposite remarks in the same categories.

The study indicated some expected, some surprising effects of integration on children's attitudes.

Emerson children were chosen at about a 2-1 advantage over Lincoln children.

Lincoln children tended to choose Emerson children and reject Lincoln children (of their own race).

Girls experienced a higher level of social belonging than boys.

Lincoln children tended to choose Emerson children on the basis of attributes and behavior, while Emerson children chose Lincoln children on the basis of relationship.

Choices tended to be built around interpersonal and play relationships. Rejections tended to center in the classroom experience.

At the end of the school year, after one semester of busing, a major study was made of the total ESEA project's first year by ESEA's coordinator and ESEA's evaluation consultant, in a 68-page report submitted to the California State Department of Education. According to the findings about the busing project gained from 420 interviews with mothers, both at the receiving and sending schools, and with teachers, "Responses pertaining to the busing program and integration of the schools reveal a strong majority approval." Eighty-one per cent of mothers of bused children, and 65 per cent of mothers of children in classes with bused children, felt it had been "good" for their children to be in contact with children from another neighborhood and another race. Only one mother from the ghetto said it had been "bad" for her child. A majority of mothers reported that their children had made new interracial friendships.

Ninety per cent of mothers of children in receiving schools, who attended classes with bused children, as well as those mothers whose children were not in classes with the newcomers, said they favored busing as a means of relieving overcrowding in other schools. Ninety-one per cent said they were for it as a means of improving learning. "The overwhelming favorable response to these questions indicates a widespread and unselfish concern for educational excellence and educational equality," the evaluator summed up.

Ninety per cent of the 420 mothers—378—had said Yes to busing. Half of them were Negro mothers, many of whom felt it was an honor for their children to be chosen to be transferred—to be regarded as sturdy enough to weather the experience. Along with their children they had taken on the busing burden when the school district asked them to be the pioneers. Among the Caucasian mothers sampled, a few truly wanted their children to have the interracial experience, but many would have chosen the "wait until" road. For the majority, I believe it was an act of faith in board and administration leadership. The board, which they had elected, had committed itself to this small first step in elementary integration. The administration had planned, discussed, and persuaded. The parents had listened, thought, argued, and gone along.

Berkeley's first busing of 238 Negro children from ghetto to the almost pure-white hills was a testing of the wind . . . an experiment . . . hopefully a showpiece of integration. Under the regulations of the federal grant financing the program, the primary aim of busing was to relieve the overcrowded classrooms of the target schools and to enhance every means of education for the resultant smaller classes in the ghetto. But in Berkeley we felt the important long run effect of busing would be on the receiving schools, not the target schools. We hoped this experiment in elementary integration would prove to our citizens that true enrichment of education comes through quality integrated schools, not through patchwork on particular schools that have been overlooked in the past.

The pilot busing project was a success as gauged by the study after six months, and another one at the end of one year of the experiment. My own judgment of its success would be positive—but. . . .

Elements of success were the rise in achievement by the Negro children bused while the achievement of their Caucasian classmates remained stable; the social impact on children of both races who, to some extent at least, stayed to play after school and visited one another's homes in hills and flats on weekends or during summer vacation; and parental acceptance to such an extent that a sizable group of Caucasian parents said they would be willing to bus their children to the Negro schools.

But there is another side to the busing story. Great loneliness accompanies the role of warriors in the cause of equality. It is not an easy role, not a light burden for young shoulders to bear. Now they see the "differences" as they ride the bus into middle Berkeley and the hills—the greener gardens, the expensive homes, the ways of living denied them in the ghetto. Now the facts of housing discrimination are engraved on their souls.

The Negro youngsters, especially the youngest among them, loved the bus ride. Robert Coles wrote in *Integrated Education* (February-March 1966): "The very bus ride gives Negro children vision, a sense of cohesion with one another, and even a feeling of pride. It is *their* bus; it is taking them places they have never seen before, places which, to them, mean a better life in the future." Their roles in their own environment are changed. "They become leaders in both their families and their neighborhoods, sources of information about the 'white world,' children who have 'been there' and return daily with stories to tell —and examples to inspire. . . ."

Nevertheless, this type of tokenism, essential as I believed this venture to be, accentuates differences. It exposes the contrast between the living patterns of the poor and the privileged; it contributes to the black and white division; it sharpens the pain of discrimination. The bus itself is a symbol of separateness, enclosing in temporary security a tightly-knit unit of Negro children who must dismount in an alien place. Perhaps busing even encourages the children to cling together as Negroes rather than mix with the whites.

Token busing also separates siblings, taking one and leaving the others down there. We were asked, again and again; "Why can't all our children be chosen? Why take one and not the others?" And it pushes down the reputation of the Negro schools. It proclaims, in effect, that the Caucasian hill schools are superior to the ghetto schools, that it is a privilege for a Negro child to be chosen to attend them. And white children, unlike the Negroes, never get a look at the other side of Berkeley—the ghetto.

All these factors were clear to us as we planned the busing move. We waited impatiently for the day when all children would attend totally integrated schools, eliminating the racial stigma of busing. This tokenism was a demonstration to speed up that day of integration. We made clear to the Negro parents involved our ultimate hopes for this experiment—we hoped it would show to all the need for, advantages of, and relative normalcy in total integration. "We *did* try to pick the youngsters who could work in well at the hill schools," Mrs. Harriett Wood, Director of Elementary Education, explained. "We did not want to perpetuate the stereotype of inferiority. We did not want to send large groups of nonachievers. We wanted the first move toward elementary integration to be successful."

An honor to be chosen, a privilege to be a pioneer in integration—this the parents and children understood and accepted. But when one or more children in a family were left behind in the ghetto schools, the experiment was harder to take.

Consider this parent of four children, who came to me for help. Two of her children were being bused to Emerson School in the hills, two remained at Lincoln in West Berkeley. She took an adamant position that all four children must attend Emerson. I explained that it was our policy to transfer siblings when vacancies occur in the receiving schools. I found it would be possible to transfer her third child but not her fourth because the grade he would attend was already overcrowded. This she would not accept. I said perhaps we could move the two children now at Emerson back to Lincoln, although we had a strict policy against transferring back. The mother could not accept this as a solution either. She liked what was happening to her children at Emerson. At Lincoln, she said, they had been getting A's, but getting them easily because they had little competition and because teachers expected less of them. At Emerson they were challenged, they had to work harder, and although they were not getting A's, as formerly, they were truly achieving. She also wanted them to continue to gain the experience of integration. She was proud of them. But why couldn't her other two children go to Emerson?

We were getting more and more such problems. We were deeply concerned that in fact we were adding to the stereotype of superiority-inferiority, reinforcing the feelings of parents whose children the bus divided that the receiving hill school was superior and soft pedalling the increasing excellence of their own schools. It was the integration experience that was superior, not the hill school. But again, if some of your children were chosen and others were not, how would you feel?

We worked for the time when we could say "Yes" to these mothers—*Yes*, all your children may take the bus, *all* your children may go to schools where integration will not be a token but an accomplished fact. We worked for the time when there would be no ghetto schools, no separation.

But the bus kept rolling, its course increasingly smooth. For the young ones, it did not start rolling too late; for the older ones, its value was not lost. It was, as we well knew, only a fragment—an experiment to point the way.

Our ESEA coordinator, put it well in a periodic report to the people.

> The busing has allowed us the chance to show that integrated education is the only quality education. The transfer program has awakened parents to the educational problems of both Negro and white ghetto schools. Segregated schools are beneficial to neither the Caucasian nor the Negro.
>
> Kids learn from each other and their environment. For the 238 bused youngsters, and for all the children in the receiving schools, the environment has been broadened.
>
> The West and South Berkeley community is greatly limited in breadth by not only the absence of Caucasians but of upper- and middle-class Negroes, many of whom have left. The children of this community come in contact only with kids of like backgrounds and experiences. They don't have contact with children of different aspirations—the word is "different," not necessarily "better."
>
> Parents volunteered their children for the busing program because they were very dissatisfied with the "separate but equal" concept of schooling.
>
> Integration will come when the Negro community no longer accepts second-class education. It will come when West and South Berkeley parents are joined by West Berkeley educators as well as educators and citizens throughout Berkeley in the demand for truly quality education, which means full, integrated, equal education for all.

11

Taxes and Integration:
A Questionable Mixture

S HOULD YOU ATTEMPT TO WIN a school tax increase while initiating a controversial integration project? This was the dilemma the Berkeley school district faced in the spring of 1966. We knew that a proposal for a much needed tax increase would come before the voters in June. Many of our strongest supporters for integration advised us that our pilot busing project would kill our chances for winning the tax increase. Some said we were out of our mind. The board and I took this to heart, but in the end decided that even the fear of losing money should not halt our progress toward integration. And so shortly after the buses began to climb up the hills, we plunged into a campaign to win the community's support for paying more taxes. It was indeed a large order. Tax increases are probably even less popular than integration, and we had had a difficult enough time winning acceptance of our busing experiment.

A well known corporation attorney headed the "Yes on G" campaign. Mrs. Carol Sibley, veteran Board of Education member, headed the main committee. The two teachers' organizations and many staff members worked intensively. Perhaps it is unusual for school personnel to work for their own tax increase. Berkeley school board members are free to do so as private citizens, of course. School staff worked only during their free time and of their free will, except for those in the Administration Building who were asked to provide facts on various issues. The teachers' organizations and the staff campaign workers, however, took their position at their own risk.

We spelled out the major needs for increased funds including reduced class size, increased teachers' salaries, a librarian for every elementary school library, expansion of the high potential program, a greatly expanded program for pre-school children, and proper maintenance and upkeep of school plants. We planned a short, only six-week campaign, to begin in mid-April. The vote would come on June 6.

The $1.50 increase we sought—bringing the school tax up to $3.25—was extremely large, much larger than increases being sought in our neighboring cities; and added to every other item of Berkeley's high cost of living (one of the highest in the United States), it must have seemed formidable to many overburdened taxpayers. Actually we had meticulously whittled the request down to our basic needs—the minimum that would maintain and expand quality education rather than cut it back. We really needed $2.75 instead of $1.50, but we settled for something less that we might realistically expect to get.

Unlike the previous campaign in 1960 for a $2.00 school tax increase which lost heavily, we did not hire a public relations firm. This was strictly a hometown campaign. We carefully avoided the Madison Avenue approach. We had only a central committee, many subcommittees, and a publicity committee, all made up of volunteers. Nobody was paid. Our slogan was simply "Yes on G." We just went out and told the truth about what our schools were doing and what they needed.

Hundreds—I'd say thousands—of us worked our heads off during that spring for "Yes on G." We worked not only our heads and our vocal chords pleading our case, but some 700 precinct workers also wore out their shoes as they campaigned from door to door. School involvement was tremendous, including board members, administrators, teachers and "classified" (non-credentialled) workers, unions and organizations that ranged from those of teachers to those of maintenance workers, the 137-member School Master Plan Committee, and the PTA's.

Civic leaders, churches, University students and faculty worked for us. Volunteers furnished most of the financial support for the campaign, and each contributed his special talents—speaking to groups or on radio or TV, painting signs, writing and distributing literature, and of course, ringing doorbells endlessly. We even had some former opponents of the Ramsey Plan working with us, and more spectacularly, some who had led the board recall movement of the fall of 1964. Alongside us also were some of those who had opposed the recent busing. This surprised and encouraged us as we worked.

The *Berkeley Daily Gazette*, which only two years before had helped initiate and had fought for the board recall, now supported the tax increase with editorials and generous news space. The *Gazette's* unexpected support may have been due to its need to regain some thousands of readers who had cancelled their subscriptions when the paper pressed for board recall in 1964—perhaps also to its belief in quality education—although not integrated. In any case, its support was welcome. The Chamber of Commerce came out for "Yes on G." The League of Women Voters supported us. We felt that the Negro community was back of us.

These were signs of hope, and publicly I said we were optimistic. Our teachers would certainly vote for higher salaries for themselves, and many citizens would be moved by the fact that our salary rate was ninth on the pay scale for the Bay Area. Parents would want the old school buildings preserved, the new ones kept up. Berkeley, the Athens of the West, the home of a great University, the chosen residence of many lovers of learning would want its gifted children to get maximum educational opportunity. They knew more money would permit smaller classes, special reading instruction, more libraries and librarians, increased early childhood education, more health and physical education. The threat of cutbacks and lowering standards was ominous to many.

But was the optimism ill-founded? Berkeley's history is not encouraging. Berkeley up to now had an unbroken record of opposition to school taxes. The 1960 win of a 75-cent tax increase, after the campaign for the needed $2.00 had lost overwhelmingly, was not truly a victory for education. In losing the larger tax increase, the board had to deny a needed raise in teachers' salaries. Many good teachers left the district and in order to attract replacements the board had then to raise salaries eight per cent, at the expense of smaller classes and adequate building maintenance.

Berkeley's conservatives were strong and numerous in 1966 as they had been in 1960. But the liberals—white and Negro—were better organized, more truly committed. The conservatives in Berkeley range from the settled wealthy and the limited-income retired, to middle and lower middle-class homeowners who are against change. Many retired teachers belong to this latter group, and want the schools to remain as they were when they were teaching— "before the Negroes came and spoiled them," as unfortunately some say. There is the area in the middle of the city, populated largely by white collar workers who feel threatened by the Negroes moving up from the flats.

We heard plenty from the fanatics. We received so many telephone calls, and so many complaining letters, that it was all we could do to accomplish our routine tasks plus pursuing the campaign. Our staff patiently answered the telephone, listening to endless tirades by those who gave their names (even some obviously made up for the moment). They opened all the letters, sorting the nut mail into the wastebasket. I began to feel as if I were back in Prince Edward County in those first days of the Free Schools.

I shall not go into all the details of a tax campaign—it was hard enough to experience it. I shall relate it only to the Berkeley scene and the process of integration. Let me tell you why many of our campaigners secretly ran scared.

School tax measures were being defeated with great regularity, not only in this area but all over the United States. There was a taxpayers' rebellion. The property taxpayer had just about had it. The nearby community of Albany, without divisive issues concerned with race, rejected a modest 50-cent increase proposal in April. How could Berkeley expect to do better with an increase three times as great?

This election represented the first time since the implementation of the Ramsey Plan that opponents had an opportunity to rap our knuckles at the polls. There were those in the community who quietly spread the word that the way to "stop Sullivan" or to "slow down the Board" was to "hit us where it hurt"—in the pocketbook. We fought this issue head-on by letting our supporters know that a defeat would be interpreted by these people as a vote of "no confidence" in the present direction of school policy and by stating that cutting off the funds necessary for a good school program for everybody was a poor and inappropriate way to express displeasure at board policies. A school board election was the forum for judging the direction the schools were going, not a needed tax increase.

We were counting on the support of the Negro community but the history of the Negro vote in Berkeley was not bright. Negro voters had not come out in large numbers. In 1960, before any integration had been achieved—or scarcely discussed—the Negroes had voted 2 to 1 against a $2.00 tax increase and, by a smaller margin, against a 75-cent compromise increase. Ironically, at that time many Negroes found themselves lined up with the then powerful Berkeley Citizens United, but from a diametrically opposite side. Negroes had considerable basis in 1960 for their opposition. A substantial bloc in the community felt the schools had not given them fair treatment, and the schools had not. One Negro citizen had issued literature and driven a sound truck up and down South and West Berkeley urging Negroes to vote against all bond and tax elections until certain wrongs were righted. He reminded the community that there were then only two Negro teachers at Berkeley High School, although 30 per cent of the student body was Negro, that tracking (grouping according to achievement level), counseling, and testing were unfair to Negroes.

There was danger of divisiveness in the Negro community now in 1966. There were still those who could be influenced by standpat or reactionary groups. And there was a split in the Negro community over two prominent and popular young Negroes running in the primary for State Assemblyman on the same ballot—John Miller, then Board of Education president, and Otho Green, head of the Neighborhood Youth Corps.

But Berkeley was far different in 1966 than it had been in 1960. Negroes generally had come to play a much more potent part in the life of the city and had made impressive contributions to various school and city commissions, committees, and organizations.

In many mass meetings to consider large community issues (the Ramsey Plan, for one) Negroes had turned out in large numbers and had the rare experience of seeing their position sustained by an elective governing board in the face of vehement opposition of middle-class hill residents. Negroes had likewise seen Berkeley take action to desegregate totally its secondary schools after extensive community and staff study. By the June, 1966, election they had also seen the ESEA funds used to provide genuine improvements in the predominantly Negro schools which their children attend and also to buy buses and use them to achieve a limited desegregation in the hill area schools. They had, in this interim, also seen real improvements in the number of Negroes employed and advanced to responsible positions in the district's administrative hierarchy. Negroes had seen the Board of Education selecting a superintendent closely identified with the civil rights cause. In sum they had seen the school district moving toward quality education for all in integrated schools.

Negroes now identified with Berkeley—and felt that Berkeley belonged to them as well as to the Caucasian residents. Hence we did not have the hostility toward the official structure, either of the school system or the city, that has prevailed in many other cities across the state and nation. In 1960 Negroes were urged to vote no as a means of expressing their displeasure with the schools; in 1966 the appeal was the reverse—Negroes were urged to vote yes, lest a defeat be interpreted as a community-wide vote of no confidence in a school system they support.

We could also predict support from the emergence of a new young group of voters, many of them UC students, 21 and over, who had become politically active. This was the New Left, its spokesman, *Ramparts,* an outstanding magazine, then new. This group formed the Community for New Politics and opposed the Viet Nam war, the draft, and discrimination against minorities. It supported movements for freedom of speech, liberalization of religion, social change in every area. The Community was running Robert

Scheer, editor of *Ramparts*, against the popular, liberal, and generally considered unbeatable incumbent Jeoffrey Cohelan in the election for United States congressman. We hoped for favorable response from these young dissenters, motivated by a strong sense of idealism on the issues of war and peace, committed to civil rights and radical social change.

But there were many "on the other hands."

Issues that imperiled our getting the needed votes had included the controversial change of attendance boundaries of the two junior high schools. Also I had supported two Berkeley teachers whose credentials were threatened by the State Credentialing Committee because they had joined the sit-in at Sproul Hall during the University of California's Freedom of Speech Movement in 1964.

Along with the public campaigning against the board and school administration, there was considerable behind-the-scenes undercutting of individuals. I was the butt of attacks ranging from my alleged manipulation of the board to the frequency with which I wear dark glasses. Some of my favorite phrases such as dialogue, innovation, and my slogan "schools worthy of imitation" were ridiculed. One prominent citizen said that every time I got up to speak, I scared "the hell" out of half the audience.

Election day coincided with our board meeting date. That night at Cragmont School, a sizable audience was there to share the suspense with us. We were almost too excited and personally apprehensive to go through the agenda. Routine reports and discussions seemed dull compared to what was going on at vote-counting headquarters. Returns were brought in to the meeting, one precinct at a time. First reports showed us slightly in the lead. We'd cheer, then turn back to the agenda. We had to wait a long time for the final answer. Finally it came. We had won by a vote of 25,341 to 16,108, by a margin of 61 to 39 per cent! John Miller, our board president, had won the State Assembly seat in the same election. In Oakland, then and now called another Watts, and in many other nearby communities, school tax increase proposals had been voted down by large majorities.

Why did we win? Because we had moved fearlessly and boldly. Because we had involved the establishment. Because we had not waited for the city's conservative segment to be persuaded. Because as educators we had taken the leadership for integration on our own shoulders. Because we had a public dialogue all the way. An informal analysis of our victory showed a substantial majority in almost every precinct. The Negroes in South and West Berkeley had given strong support because they had seen substantial gains being made for them in the schools. The University campus area, usually a low-voting section, came through with an unusually high vote for us. Every political party, including the New Left, was represented in our support.

We could call it a vote for integration. Those who had urged a "No" vote to slow us down had not succeeded. Those who had attacked us personally had not diminished us. We had not skirted controversial issues during the pre-election year, we had hidden nothing from the voters, we had made no deals, and therefore we were free of hostages.

We had emerged with a reputation for being honest about what we had done and what we planned to do, in spite of political pressures. We could call it a smashing vote of confidence. The victory left our opponents in total disarray. Most encouraging of all was the proof that South and West Berkeley and a scattering of other minorities were with us.

My post-election statement to the press reflected my mood of jubilance and gratitude: "The overwhelming endorsement of our schools by Berkeley citizens is indicative of the commitment here for programs *administered for the benefit of the entire community.* Berkeleyans have hearts and minds which will rally to support programs, both new and old, when their advantages and disadvantages are openly presented, discussed, and reviewed."

That is my belief. I saw that minds had changed; I felt that hearts had changed also.

I believe strongly too that Berkeley parents had been influenced by their children. They had not seen their 12 to 14 year-olds suffer under the Ramsey Plan, nor their elementary school children marred by contact with the bused children. In the end integration had involved no trauma, no fuss. Our parents now had some real experience with integration, not just talk about integration, and they understood it better. We want to continue, they said at the polls June 6.

We want to continue. I believe that meant to continue forging ahead toward total integration. We could mark time for years with the experimental, limited one-way busing, but I interpreted this community support for us through the pocketbook as a mandate. A mandate to move rapidly to our stated ultimate goal—quality integrated education.

12

Cool Summer of Tax Victory

THE SUMMER OF 1966 WAS INDEED COOL—in physical as well as emotional climate. When anyone asked, "How're you doing?", our answer was "Just fine!" We went to work investing the added tax funds in the needed areas. Teachers' salaries were raised; summer sessions, which we had feared would have to be curtailed, were held as usual; early childhood education was expanded; the foreign language program was enlarged; the high potential program was broadened; improved maintenance of buildings was begun. We worked at both ends of the educational spectrum— improving the opportunities for gifted and high potential students and developing better basic skills among our disadvantaged children and slow learners.

We expanded our high potential program at least threefold. We named one of our dynamic young staff members, who had worked alone and valiantly in teaching the gifted, as coordinator of a program with four specially trained teachers to work directly with the gifted children. We employed a full-time psychologist to identify gifted children not yet discovered and to counsel their parents. At the elementary school level alone, we had identified during the past school year 430 students with IQ's of 130 or above. We knew there were many more throughout the city, from hills to ghetto—at least 10 per cent of the public school population was in the top 2 per cent of the nation in ability. Now we could mine this great store of riches which we had only tapped. The high potential teachers spent the summer developing programs for the gifted and developing new study materials that would meet and challenge young minds. Among them, for example, were an architecture project in which the fourth-grade children would do mockups and models of homes or buildings suiting their dreams; a musical session of composing blues fitted into a third-grade math class; a plan for sixth-graders to make a local survey of teenage attitudes; and a wide variety of units in art, poetry, and music.

We were also appraising and expanding Project SEED (Special Elementary Education for the Disadvantaged), which William Johntz, a young high school math teacher, had started in 1963. Johntz had used his lunch periods and "planning time" to initiate an experiment with a group of fifth-grade children in the ghetto schools. The children were selected by their teachers, not necessarily as children who had tested out with high IQ's or who were high all-around achievers or good steady behavers, but as exhibiting high potential in the teachers' views. Among these children, disadvantaged by ghetto conditions, Johntz found fifth-graders who could solve algebraic intangibles at university level. Followup studies showed that these children's reading scores have gone up impressively, their IQ scores have risen 21 points, and their grade equivalent has advanced 2 years.

Now Johntz, through the cooperation of the University of California with the School District, could put in full time on Project SEED, and with eleven math specialists from UC and other universities, could conduct 17 classes in this program. Although the appraisal of SEED is still subjective, news of this project has spread through California and the nation. Scholars have been very enthusiastic about the project so far. Owen Chamberlain, a professor of physics and Nobel Prize winner, said, "It is, to begin with, very promising from a purely philosophical point of view because of the choice of an area of study in which the so-called disadvantaged are not any more disadvantaged than anyone else." Daniel A. Collins, a member of the California State Board of Public Education, made the following conclusions: 1) It completely dispels the myth which one has been led to believe that these children "can't think in the abstract," 2) The illusion that the children "can't concentrate" proves a lie. I would add that with programs like SEED carried out in an integrated classroom the term "disadvantaged" would soon die away.

That summer, while elated by the possibilities for SEED, we were also working—with some of that tax money—on the problem of the Negro student at the other end of the achievement scale, the student found "able but achieving below his ability." In the secondary schools we have four tracks or achievement levels, geared to the student's pace in learning. For many reasons every reader knows—poverty, discrimination, insecurity, low self-image —many Negro students fall into the lower tracks. They are unequal again, labeled and diminished. Yet the learning pace of higher achievers must not be held back.

Tracking is a real problem and I shall give a whole chapter to it shortly. We are working on it. What we planned that summer, for implementation in the fall, was to assign a few teachers in each secondary school to identify and work individually with minority students who, by tutoring and support, could move up into higher tracks.

That summer wound toward fall in an atmosphere of optimism for us. The busing of the 238 Negro children to primarily white schools had proved quietly successful. In fact some parents, both Negro and white, wanted us to expand it. The Ramsey Plan of integrating seventh, eighth and ninth graders was smoothing out problems and was getting better all the time. White parents' complaints had become negligible. And in the ghetto schools ESEA funds had brought about great improvement through smaller classes, imaginative programs, more effective teaching.

Only one incident marred the peaceful progress of our summer. It foreshadowed the growing Black Power movement in the Bay Area. One of the directors of the Bay Area Economic Opportunity Board—a white resident of West Berkeley—circulated a flier before a large public meeting at San Pablo Park Recreation Center—a meeting at which the ESEA plan to continue the busing of 238 children from ghetto to hill schools was discussed. "WHITE IS NOT RIGHT," declared this director in his dramatic leaflet. The busing, he charged, robs West Berkeley schools of their best material. Spend the busing money to improve the ghetto schools—the playgrounds, the libraries. Keep the money in the ghetto. Forget about mixing with whites. Keep the kids down here. "West Berkeley is worth three times the white hills."

Franklin School parents—two of them connected with the same Equal Opportunities Board—rose and denounced the agitator at the meeting. One Board of Education member suggested censure for publication of such a missive without permission of the Economic Opportunity Board, whose members obviously did not agree on its contents. The author of "White is Not Right" was so soundly censured that one Negro teacher questioned the embarrassment he was caused by such a direct confrontation. But she was the only one. The audience was against him and did not hesitate to say so.

Later I asked our Director of Elementary Education to get statements from the numerous parents who had spoken out. That meeting and those statements told us we were right, that the parents of South and West Berkeley were with us. They declared for busing and more of it, for Head

Start, for neighborhood workers, for more parent participation, for more programs for the gifted.

Berkeley kept its cool and marched ahead. But then came the September hot spell—a stifling, smoggy spell that reminded us of Watts and its riots there the year before. Now we too faced the heat.

13

A Hot Fall: Race Riots
Echo in Berkeley

I N THE BAY AREA there comes in September a hot spell—
stiflingly, smoggily hot—and nobody is prepared for it.
Everybody suffers and waits tensely for the cool fog to
drift in from the sea. In late September, 1966, the Negro
and Mexican-American slums of nearby Hunter's Point in
San Francisco exploded. It was not Watts, to be sure, but
a tragic confrontation and one that reverberated in our
schools in Berkeley. Again, as in Watts, it was the minority
youth, the jobless high school students and high school
dropouts, who burst out in anger.

"It grimly dramatized," wrote the *San Francisco Chron-
icle,* "that Negro frustration and anger were no different in
the supposedly tolerant, sophisticated Queen of the West
than it was in the teeming black ghettos of the East and
Midwest. A proud, smug city was shocked out of its illusion."

Neither was it basically different in Berkeley, the
Athens of the West, and our illusions too were shattered
when minor violence burst out in our schools. Although we
knew that violence in any city can spark violence in others,
Berkeley, we thought, was different. We have the same
roots of violence, the same racism, the same discrimination
in housing and employment. But the ghetto in Berkeley
was not a smoldering slum that can be compared to Hunter's Point; Negro leadership was growing stronger; our city

government and police force were relatively tolerant and wise, and our schools were becoming integrated. At this time, the beginning of the third year of secondary school desegregation, hostile incidents between black and white youth at school had diminished and progress generally had been reassuring. But in spite of its superior circumstances, its calm surface, Berkeley was not immune.

Hunter's Point in San Francisco, primarily populated by poor Negroes and Mexican-Americans, is one of the most beautiful hill areas in the city. Its full name is Hunter's Point-Bayview and tourists and residents alike drive up there just to see the view. But up to now they had gazed only at the placid bay, looking beyond the shocking hillside slum in which people lived—the tumble-down, rat-ridden housing, the discrimination, the unemployment, the despair, the smoldering anger. When a policeman's bullet killed a 16-year-old Negro boy in Hunter's Point, the rage and frustration that had bred and festered there, burst forth. Forty-two persons were injured, many jailed.

In Berkeley, the day after the Hunter's Point riots began—20 to 30 Negro boys at West Campus started shouting and shoving at a school assembly. One boy, claiming relationship to the boy killed at Hunter's Point, added fuel to the outburst. The next day, three Caucasian students were struck by Negroes on their way to school and four others were struck on the school grounds. Nobody was seriously hurt physically. Only one boy suffered lacerations.

While the heat was still on at Hunter's Point, some West Campus Negro youths came to the Berkeley High campus after a football game to vent their hostility. Two white students were punched and a coke bottle was thrown through a bus window. On Friday at the high school some 60 Negro high school students gathered after school, chanting "Black Power," and made their way into several science laboratories and, when rebuffed by several white students, struck them.

In San Francisco Mayor John Shelley had spoken out impressively. He did not place the blame; he did not seek to punish. He faced facts, accepted his responsibility, and called upon the citizens of the community to understand and do the same. He sought to galvanize the community, to improve and correct the conditions that had caused the violence. However, as many asked, why had he waited to speak until after violence?

Glossing over San Francisco's outburst, as well as our comparatively minor outburst in Berkeley, would be as dangerous as treating cancer with an aspirin. Now was the time for exploration in depth of the disease for which the current eruptions of hate, anger, threats and violence were merely the symptoms. Now was the time to explore not only what we have done that this should happen, but what we have failed to do.

I did not wait for school to open on Monday. Sunday afternoon a group of students and teachers telephoned, then came to my home to express their concern over what had happened and the effect of these events in our schools. I was deeply impressed by their suggestions and the questions to which they wanted answers. I talked with them at great length, then called an emergency meeting of our top administrative staff. From 7 o'clock that evening until midnight, we reviewed what the young people had told me and discussed what action we could take.

We called a meeting at the high school for Monday afternoon, October 3, to bring the whole situation into the open—to hear from the students, the student leaders, and to answer as best we could. Why had this happened here? What were the root causes? What could we do? What must we do?

First, Emery Curtice, Berkeley High School principal,

and Carl Dwight, West Campus principal, reported exactly what had happened. They reported minutely and objectively, with pain in their voices. Curtice, grieved because our distinguished high school, its excellence marked by many awards, was now in trouble. Dwight, because his "all-14-year-olds," who had seemed to be getting along so well together, had burst into hostility.

The students were striking in their candor. They did not spare us as they told us "like it is." They both denounced us and made constructive suggestions. Several Negro students struck out sharply, saying "I't's time for Whitey to get his!" and "We're tired of waiting, now we're out for action!"

And we listened. The main gripe was tracking. "That old bag!" they exclaimed. "The smart white kids get steered up into the top tracks, the black kids down into the 'dumb' tracks. The Negro girls can take Homemaking and maybe music. All they want the girls to do is learn how to cook and sew and maybe sing! The Negro boys can go down in the shop to run the saws and push the buttons!"

They pleaded: "We want to have ambition but we don't know where to get it."

Black and white students asked for a place to air their grievances—a comfortable place of their own, away from teachers—where both races could get together, air their gripes, and plan ways to do something about it. They want a place, they said, to express their "hurts," to "get out our emotions." Negro students urged the teaching of Negro history—"taught fairly" in American History classes.

It was a healthy meeting. We administrators were deeply impressed by the student's statements, and we understood the anger some expressed. We had made headway by this confrontation. We had paved the way for true communication. But, as one of the principals said, "It's what happens now that's crucial."

Emery Curtice went immediately to work with the high school students to provide that "comfortable" place for airing "gripes" that the students asked for. The Interracial Club set up the year before was the nucleus for expansion. A grievance committee "that can really work" was set up.

And now our staff got busy on the "frustration" of the tracking system, a problem with which we had been deeply concerned, but which was not a simple one to change or to change quickly.

Late that evening student leaders called me at home to report their satisfaction with the meeting. We had listened carefully, they said, and we had made promises. The student body as a whole would be reassured, would feel students had a voice, would feel we were with them. I also received many letters, most of them approving, even laudatory. This one, from Reverend James Keeley of St. Joseph's Church, truly expressed, I hoped, what we had been accomplishing in the Berkeley schools: "Congratulations on Monday's session with students, press, TV, faculty, etc. Theologians talk about 'The *Open* Church.' I venture to say that Berkeley schools have the same spirit of honesty and frankness."

A few days later I published in the weekly column I write for the Berkeley paper a report of my reactions to the meeting, summing up the essence of the meeting as I saw and felt it.

Although no problems were solved immediately, and although it may take time to implement some of the improvements we hope to make, I consider Monday's meeting a success because it clearly indicated our sincere interest in keeping the lines of communication open. The students were heard and they heard us. We understand each other.

My colleagues, Berkeley's excellent teaching staff, my administrators, and I are fully cognizant of our responsibilities and accept the full burden of them. However, students and parents and all of the people involved in changing and improving our schools, our city, our society, must also accept the responsibility for their own behavior and actions.

I feel that the problem is not to *do for* our troubled youth—the problem is to establish a rapport and understanding and work together with youth, *each sharing personal and community responsibilities.*

Violence was the symptom, tracking was one of the diseases—a chronic disease that could not be cured quickly, nor wiped out overnight as the impatient students hoped. We intensified our work toward means to alleviate tracking, and while we worked we held meetings where students and parents opened up on violence. It was clear we had a long way to go.

14

Whose Violence?

Now I want to talk about violence.
I am tired of hearing about school integration as
the main cause of racial violence. I am tired of Caucasian
parents who come to board members, or to me, to tell us
—after the fact—of incidents of violence, threats of violence, "bumming" or "shakedowns" experienced by their
children, and to demand that the schools do something
about it.

Violence is and has been a part of life in every ghetto
for centuries—even in all-white ghettos, as Gorki's *Lower
Depths* and Eugene Sue's *Streets of Paris* told us long ago.
Now we see some of that violence naturally spilling over
into integrated schools. Integration is not the cause; it exposes the phenomenon. And integration can be the cure.

Violence is a fact. "Why don't we do something about
it?" parents demand. Do something? We are doing something. We face it, incident by incident, as it explodes. Let
me say again that integration does not cause, does not increase violence. It transfers the scene of action and exposes
its causes. We see integration as a major attack on violence.

Current writers suggest that real violence comes only
after the apathy of poverty is lifted and hope of a better
life reaches into the ghetto. The tardy beginning to fulfillment of that hope sparks violence and rebellion out of the

ghetto dweller's impatience. The Negro ghetto has no monopoly on violence. Many of us who grew up in the ghetto—Irish, Negro, Jewish, or other—made our way with our fists, feet, and elbows. But if we were white kids, and if our parents were able to push their way up economically, we could get up into the middle-class schools where we learned to restrain or sublimate.

Let me quote from a *Time* magazine essay on "Violence in America" (July 28, 1967):

> Violence is not only an urban but overwhelmingly a lower-class phenomenon. In Atlanta, for example, neighborhoods with family incomes below $3,000 show a violent-crime rate eight times higher than among $9,000 families. In the middle class, violence is perhaps sublimated increasingly in sport or other pursuits. Says Sociologist [Marvin E.] Wolfgang [in *Subculture of Violence*]: "The gun and fist have been substantially replaced by financial ability, by the capacity to manipulate others in complex organizations, and by intellectual talent." The thoughtful wit, the easy verbalizer, even the striving musician and artist are equivalents of male assertiveness, where broad shoulders and fighting fists were once the major symbols.

And again from the same article, "Violence is not power. In the last analysis it is an admission of failure, a desire for a magical shortcut, an act of despair."

This country's tremendous task is to eliminate the ghetto. When this is accomplished alienation and violence will dissolve. For school boards and superintendents the task is to get the children out of the ghetto, out of isolation into the major world; to give them an equal chance to learn with other social classes, to provide them with other means than violence to express themselves.

In Berkeley we have been able to begin this process—first desegregation, then, increasingly, true integration.

We have begun and are continuing not because of our

fear of or reaction to violence, but because the majority knows integration is right and has moved peacefully into carefully planned action. With all children—of every color, creed, and social class—together under one roof, mixed in every classroom, integration begins. Principals, teachers, children *build* integration, not all at once but step by step.

Part of the process is facing together, or in groups, the fact of violence. Why is there violence and threatened violence among us? With whom did the violence begin? On whom has the violence fallen since slavery began and ended? The children are thinking about these questions as they study Negro History and meet in student councils and discussion clubs. They are getting at the roots of violence.

The whites have much to learn about violence. Negroes today know that resigned acceptance of unjust acts is not the appropriate response. It is no help to the school's efforts to maintain a peaceful environment when children accept incidents of violence, of shakedowns or bumming— when they cower or retreat or give in. It is no help to a child for his mother to come to take him home for lunch or to pick him up after school, thus to pamper and protect him. Youngsters have got to "equal with each other," "level with each other," as one student so wisely expressed it.

A conversation I had with some board members went to the heart of the problem. Board members were receiving complaints about shakedowns and threats of violence by Negro students at the junior high schools. The white students, they heard, were intimidated by their Negro associates. One board member reported that a highly respected neighbor of his had told him that his daughter had a frightening experience; naturally he did not like it and he wanted the school to make sure it did not happen again. I asked this board member if his friend or his daughter had reported the incident to the principal, the dean, or the teacher. No. He had not reported it because if he had done so, retaliation against his daughter would have resulted.

"Your friend is not my idea of an honorable citizen," I told the board member. "As a matter of fact, he's a dead citizen. Why didn't he go to the principal, if his child was scared to go? Was he scared too? It's his kind of attitude that in the long run will be extremely damaging to all and to the causes we are fighting for in this community and this country." Why do we persist in accepting stereotypes? How can we accept the irrational position that *all* Negroes are violent?

At this point the Reverend Hazaiah Williams, board member and a Negro, pastor of the liberal, interracial Church for Today, joined in. Caucasians, both children and adults, may have to do a little suffering as we move ahead with integration, he said. He pointed out that the Negroes have faced the problems alone for more than 100 years and they have been paying the price. He said the Negroes will go on paying the price but that the Caucasians must understand that they, too, must pay a price for the sins of the past. He declared that it was about time parents made it clear to children that the problems we have in the community are not going to be solved overnight and that the schools are not going to be able to solve them alone. We must all work together—schools and parents, community and schools, said the Reverend Williams.

In the Berkeley schools, I would estimate that a vast majority of the Negro children were trying to avoid violence. Parents tend to forget that there was trouble in all-white schools, that there were all-white gangs, long before integration began. Violence and potential violence *exist* in both races—white and Negro.

I do not believe we should condone or explain away violence, however. Every incident of bumming, shake-

down, intimidation, or threat by a child—Negro or white
—must be reported at once to a teacher, principal, or other
adult authority. The child himself, whether he's a liberal
white child afraid he might get a Negro in trouble or a
Negro frightened to tell on a white child, should do the
reporting. If he's not up to it, his parents should immediately report it. We don't end trouble by concealing it but
by facing it. Every student, every teacher, every parent
who sees or hears about a lock being jimmied, a window
broken, a child struck or arm-twisted or threatened, should
speak out. Is this cowardice? Squealing? No, it is courage;
it is good citizenship. A good citizen will not be silent in
the face of injustice or destruction.

The plain fact is—and this has been documented in our
schools—retaliation is an overworked and outworn fear. In
our secondary schools, almost all principals have been able
to handle incidents of trouble successfully. When reported
promptly, faced quietly, the trouble ends and is not soon, if
ever, repeated.

The students themselves are handling it best, and learning and growing in the process. In the Student Relations
Councils and the afterschool discussion clubs in the secondary schools minority and majority youngsters together
face the problems and talk them out, make recommendations and enforce them, write about them in their school
papers. Problem-facing is going on also in the elementary
schools, where increasingly they are organizing student
governments and discussion groups that concern themselves with everything from how many hot dogs to take to
a picnic to serious matters of behavior. In one elementary
school—grades 4-6—the upper-grade children are helping
enforce the disciplinary rules.

The retreats I have described are tremendously valuable. They are limited, of course, because attendance is
voluntary, including only those with the courage and

stamina to share this candid, probing experience. The young people come back to school, Negro and white together, friends and leaders in pursuit of interracial harmony and understanding. They know that integration is not a simple nor easy process. They know that rules and policies and mandates saying "Don't do that!" are not the answer. Open facing of problems, exploration of roots and causes, are the way.

With parents, teachers, principals and the superintendent back of them in the integrated school, the boys and girls—black and white—will work it out together.

15

Tracking, "That Old Bag," Must Go

I N BERKELEY'S SECONDARY SCHOOLS, as in those of many cities, we have faced this difficult dilemma: Do the educational advantages claimed for tracking (grouping students according to achievement level) outweigh its striking side-effect—segregation within schools, even in desegregated schools? Can a school system be fair to all students, learning at various levels, without some form of ability grouping?

As the black students here protest against tracking and many white students back their protest, the answer has to be No. No, the educational advantages of tracking do not outweigh the segregation-within-desegregation that results. Tracking must be eliminated. It must be eliminated step-by-step, but the steps must be taken quickly. In Berkeley, on May 21, 1968, we initiated these steps. I recommended, and the board approved, interim steps to be taken in September, 1968, and major changes for February, 1969, with the expressed hope that we could see the end of tracking in 1970.

Berkeley schools have had three major confrontations on tracking. In 1963, the Citizens Committee on Discrimination, established in response to demands by CORE and NAACP, moved toward recommendations that resulted in secondary school desegregation in September, 1964. The committee charged that the tracking system fostered rigid intraschool class and race segregation, and its report gave significant insights on the problem. At that time the Berkeley secondary schools had up to 15 tracks, depending on the enrollment at a given grade level at a given date.

On May 19, 1964—four months before secondary desegregation went into effect, the board diminished the tracks to four. The board's action was hailed as outstanding, as the best possible solution in fairness to all children and the variety in which they come.

This was the board policy then established:

Students in these sections (classes) do not differ in kind; they differ in the degree to which they are capable of handling abstract thought, literary allusions, subtleties of style, and complexity of sentence structure.

Students grow at irregular rates; therefore, placement in tracks must be tentative and flexible. At the end of any report period students may be moved from one track to another. Occasionally they may be moved between report periods if a teacher finds that some mistake in placement has been made. This applies to every track.

Students in grades 7-12 shall be placed in one of four broad achievement groups for each academic subject; a deliberate attempt shall be made to integrate students within the same achievement groups. No hierarchy of classes shall be set up within this achievement group structure. . . .

The purpose of grouping and tracking is to provide for individual differences, to offer equal opportunity for all students to strive to reach their potential regardless of what the potential may be.

Students had been assigned to the tracks in secondary schools by two processes. The State of California requires tests of all sixth-grade students as they prepare to enter junior high schools. The test results form one criteria for placement. Second, and more importantly, the student's sixth-grade teacher who, before the final lists for grouping are compiled, is given at least two opportunities to react to and to recommend the assignment. According to board policy, the sixth-grade teacher's recommendation determines initial placement in seventh grade.

In Berkeley we are highly critical of the standard tests the state requires. We find them unfair to many minority and poor children. Generally, they are geared to middle-class white experience, and their wording and imagery can be confusing and unrealistic to other children. Our teachers and psychologists do all they can to help the sixth-graders over the testing hurdle. They prepare the students for the general nature of the tests and explain their relevance to the student's future. They provide an informal and personalized setting in which the tests are given. Every attempt is made to avoid tension and create rapport.

Generally, the tracks established in September, 1964, following the board's action, formed around English, Science, Music and Art, and Social Science. The rationale was that in these areas all students cannot work at the same pace—cannot perform the same experiments in the labs, tackle the same abstractions in math, cannot grasp the same language concepts. We instructed the teachers to keep the tracks flexible and do their utmost to move students up wherever and whenever possible. Many volunteer tutors helped the upward move; they included School Resource Volunteers (SRVs), a district organization that draws as many as 500 community adults and university students into service, other parent volunteers, and junior high school student-tutor volunteers.

A study of 239 students completing the first semester of the new four-track system confirmed our feeling that any tracking was doomed to result in segregation. Over 50 per cent of the white students were in track 1 as compared with 18 per cent of the Negro students. Track 2 contained about 30 per cent of the white students and 26 per cent of the Negroes. But over 50 per cent of the Negroes were in tracks 3 and 4 as compared with approximately 16 per cent of the white students. Academic subjects—English, Mathematics, Science and Social Studies were those measured.

During that first year of the new four-track system, I insisted that home rooms, music and art and drama, physical education classes be heterogeneous massing of all students. In all secondary schools we launched pilot programs, some on a fairly large scale, to break down tracking in certain areas. Those found successful were expanded.

But this major effort was not enough. In October, 1966, we arrived at and had to meet our second confrontation in the wake of San Francisco Hunter's Point riots and Berkeley's Negro student minor explosion. Tracking was the main gripe. It was the symbol of discrimination that constantly prodded their bitterness and anger. We were vulnerable. We pledged more flexibility, we went back to the Administration Building to study what more we could do.

Meanwhile a report came out of the School Master Plan Committee which we had organized in early 1965 after secondary desegregation had begun and the board recall move defeated. The committee was charged with taking the schools apart and recommending how to put them together in a model pattern for short-range and long-range development. The committee called for the end of tracking. It declared that tracking "constitutes a violation of our moral, educational and legal commitment to integrated schools." It stated that a student's classmates play a most important role in determining his intellectual progress. "It is unreasonable to expect a low-achieving student to pick up more favorable attitudes if his classroom contacts are limited to other students with low motivation and aspirations." Remember the Negro student who told us, "I want to have ambition but I don't know where to get it."

Now we tried harder. Administrators worked on plans for change. Teacher tutoring was expanded. A few teachers were freed to devote all their time to tutoring. Efforts were made by teachers and counselors to identify promising but under-achieving students, place them in higher tracks and give them tutorial help to make it in those tracks. One of several programs at one of our junior high schools moved 25 promising Negro students from track 2 to track 1 in seventh-grade English. To help them succeed, five teachers were freed one period each day, to work with five students each.

At another junior high school, one completely heterogeneous group was organized in seventh-grade science and one in seventh-grade math, involving 50 students. Later two groups from tracks 2 and 3—over 100 students—were merged in history and English. Teachers committed to the effort volunteered. Parents were called in to give their consent and cooperation.

Many teachers worked on their own after school, helping minority students with reading, math, or whatever their weak subject, making it possible to move them up a track. And students tutored students. At one junior high school, honor students and others in the upper tracks helped their classmates. At Berkeley High School, Negro student leaders (who emerged later as the Black Student Union) worked intensively to get less able and less interested students to hit the books.

Could we eliminate tracking at this time? It seemed impossible. We were molding consensus for total elementary integration in the spring of 1966, yet many of our supporters pressed us to undertake the other necessary revolution—elimination of secondary school tracking—at one and the same time. Could we begin at the end—the secondary desegregated schools where racial segregation had long been the pattern—and at the beginning, with young children as yet uncontaminated by discrimination, at one and the same time?

I learned long ago that you can win only one battle at a time. In New York I learned that I could move toward a nongraded system and team-teaching only after teachers had learned to work together. In spring, 1964, the board had tabled "indefinitely" elementary integration plans because of their dread of busing. To me and to the present board "indefinitely" meant until secondary integration was complete. Now that we had reached that point we had to move quickly. Progress once begun must accelerate. Elementary integration by busing was a much greater undertaking on which to gain community consensus than the Ramsey Plan. One revolution at a time—that was my thinking as we moved for Integration 1968 through the elementary schools. Tracking could not be uprooted as Integration 1968 began.

Then came the death of Martin Luther King, the overwhelming grief, the anger, and the demand from black students for "Change Now!" Our third confrontation. We could wait no longer to begin to destroy "that old bag tracking." We would have to do both things at once. The role of our schools, of our boards of education, of our superintendents, is to produce change. Now in Berkeley we must produce it on two fronts.

Out of our intensive study of tracking change, out of days and nights of concentrated thought, we came up with a program. At the board meeting of May 21, 1968, I presented a two-stage program which the board approved. In the fall track 4 (what the students term the dumb track) was to be dropped, leaving three tracks in grades seven through twelve. Tracks 1 through 3 were retained in all subjects except seventh and eighth grade social studies. Social studies would be ungrouped. Honors sections in grades seven and eight were merged into track 1, providing independent study, special seminars, and opportunity to be excused from work already mastered, for gifted students. Teachers or teams of teachers who wanted to teach ungrouped classes were encouraged to do so, provided the curriculum met standards, that parental permission to participate in such classes was granted, and the classes were evaluated.

As of February, 1968, "open enrollment" was offered to students desiring to move up into a higher track, based on consultation among the student, parent, teachers, and counselors. Final decision would rest with the student and his parents. Additional remedial reading services were provided for students reading below grade level. Subject-oriented study halls were provided for those who were weak in basic skills. For those teachers desiring it, team-teaching blocks were scheduled. Increased tutorial help by teachers and volunteers was made available.

I applaud this interim program. I see it as the beginning of the end of "that old bag tracking." Our teachers, in spite of the problems ungrouped teaching entails for them, have helped lead the move to end it. I believe the new program will work if they can meet its demands for understanding, imagination, skill, and hard work. I believe it will work if the minority students turn that angry energy that the event of Martin Luther King's death released into study. I believe it will work if parents, teachers, and administrators stand firmly behind them.

16

Face-to-Face on Prejudice: Teaching Teachers

Prejudice is a disease that may never fully disappear but the crippling effects are curable. If adults think nothing can be done they won't try. But if they try, they're likely to accomplish something.

THAT IS DR. BENJAMIN SPOCK SPEAKING—Dr. Spock, a pediatrician and psychiatrist who has profoundly influenced a generation of babies, speaking on a television program in 1967, "The Victims," a study of the effects of racial prejudice.

In Berkeley an assault on prejudice began in 1960 through the Berkeley school district's Intergroup Education Project, which has since been a model for many other school districts and communities in California and other states. "We work with the hearts and minds of teachers, parents and youngsters," says Mrs. Kathryne Favors, Intergroup's coordinator.

Intergroup grew out of the 1959 report by a citizens' committee to the Board of Education on "Interracial Problems and Their Effect on Education in the Public Schools of Berkeley, California." One recommendation asked for a review of our textbooks and curriculum to see if the contributions of minority groups were covered adequately and to remedy any deficiencies found. A second recommendation asked for intergroup education for the school staff. The following fall, Dr. Marie Fielder of the University of California's School of Education was employed by the district as director-consultant in intergroup relations. Dr. Fielder, a dynamic woman who can get a group moving with more power and grace than almost anyone I ever saw in action, started a once-a-week seminar for teachers on "Cultural Influences on Learning." Fifteen pioneer teachers signed up. The next year, 120 teachers sat down with Dr. Fielder and other leaders, including Mrs. Favors, who became head of the project. Seminars were soon opened up to the public and at this writing several thousand Berkeleyans— teachers and others—are involved. A community-wide Friends of the Intergroup Education Project was organized in 1966.

Seminars cover every minority—its problems and progress, its contributions—but because Berkeley's prevailing minority is Negro, the dominant focus has been on this group. Teachers who participate are given in-service credit. New teachers are encouraged to take the basic seminar which covers Negro history and minority group problems and contributions. Intergroup also sponsored a group of special seminars and groups who go on field trips, produce dramas, and study legislation concerning minority problems. Intergroup has also introduced "Leadership Training" for staff members in administrative positions. In the 1967-1968 school year, Intergroup's focus was on preparing schools and community for elementary school integration in September, 1968.

Intergroup is a resource for literature, for speakers, and for consultation. It has published a manual of sources, materials and projects. For the schools it provides a mobile library. Its Drama Seminar has presented its production "Walking the Earth Like Men" to some 10,000 people. Its field trip group explores Bay Area productions relating to intergroup problems, or featuring Negro performers, and brings many distinguished Negroes—actors, jazz artists, singers, painters, writers—to school auditoriums. Marion Anderson has come three times.

Throughout our desegregation progress—during the Ramsey Plan's beginnings, the ESEA token busing of 238 Negro children to white schools, and the preparation for total integration in 1968—Intergroup has been a key agency in preparing schools and community.

When Intergroup Education Project holds one of its community assemblies, which it does almost every year, teachers and other concerned citizens pour in from other districts and other states in overflow crowds. One such was the "Community Assembly on Negro History and Literature" mentioned in an earlier chapter; another, "Creating Intelligence," was a lively discussion of the unfair elements in testing.

Intergroup worked with teaching specialists to produce a textbook and guide called "The History of the Negro in America," used in a unit introduced into all fifth grades in Berkeley in February, 1967. The children learn for the first time that many groups of people, not just Negroes, come from tribal backgrounds; that almost all people have been slaves at one time; and that the first Negroes who came to America were explorers, not slaves. It tells of the many contributions Negroes have made to our democratic society through all our struggles and throughout the building of our culture.

Berkeley is the only school district, or one of a very few, that has incorporated the history of African and American Negroes at all levels of its schools. We begin in the social studies classes in the first grade in such projects as "The American Family," and we continue right on through high school. Negro history classes are offered as electives and attended by both black and white students at Berkeley High School and East Campus (a continuation high school for potential dropouts—students who cannot meet the requirements and cannot adjust to the main high school.) African and American Negro history is incorporated into United States history I, II, and III in grades ten through twelve; into sociology at grade ten; into world history in grade nine at West Campus; into United States history in grade eight, and into world geography in grade seven. For many years we have had a course in Negro History at Berkeley Adult School. We are changing the names of these classes to Black or Afro-American History, which many Negro students now prefer.

As the unit in Negro History began in the fifth grades, Intergroup offered the same course, geared for adults, to principals and administrative staff, from parent nursery and pre-school center staff through high school. The course was consolidated into four sessions and was enthusiastically received. Some wanted to refresh their knowledge, others recognized the need for more awareness, and all needed to keep pace with fifth grade teachers and students.

Intergroup, with the help of service clubs, annually introduces new teachers to the community in September. The new teachers, with Intergroup, Kiwanis, and a Chamber of Commerce guide, ride buses from the hills to the Bay, while representatives from the three groups take turns briefing the new teachers on Berkeley's geography, ecology and culture.

It has been a long-standing policy of the Berkeley district to work toward an integrated staff at every school. The district has come a long way since 1944 when the first two Negro teachers were hired and then relegated to kindergarten posts in spite of their training for another age level.

By 1966 Berkeley's record showed 19 per cent minority teachers, 13.5 per cent of whom were Negroes. On a statewide basis 25 per cent of California's schoolchildren in 1966 were from minority groups, while the percentage of minority teachers was only 11 per cent. Most shocking of the statistics showed that while 13.7 per cent of the pupils bore Spanish surnames and only 2.5 per cent of the teachers shared their heritage. Negroes composed 8.6 per cent of California's pupils and only 4.5 per cent of the teachers in 1967.

By 1968 Berkeley's Negro teacher proportion had gone up to 17.5 per cent. Now our percentage is rising higher. But our task is not easy. As integration goes into action, we have had to send teams of teachers and personnel staff throughout the country, particularly to the southern and southwestern states, to recruit Negro teachers. Why is it that so few Negroes have gone into teacher training in the north? Few have been encouraged and the financial rewards in industrial employment are much greater. California was jolted by the shocking 1966 figures on the proportions of minority teachers, and the state board immediately asked its Commission on Equal Opportunity in Education to take steps to correct the situation. The most promising suggestion made was for "full circle" scholarships to encourage minority youth to enter teacher training institutions, and the idea has since been developed on the federal level. The State Fair Employment Practices Commission pledged its cooperation in this effort to train Negro teachers. The University is now recruiting Negro teacher candidates strenuously. But California has a long way to go.

So far as integration of our own teachers is concerned, we are far from Utopia. We still have some rigid teachers who have not fully accepted desegregation, who keep carefully apart from Negro teachers, who inwardly and sometimes outwardly resent the presence of Negro students in their formerly all-white classrooms. In most cases, but not all, they are teachers who have long taught only middle-class white children, who somehow have not known Negroes and who have a white middle-class hangup. Some can change, and some cannot.

In Berkeley we try never to hire a prejudiced teacher. Our personnel director is experienced at tapping prejudice. He has had 4,000 applications annually in recent years, among them the cream of the crop. Berkeley attracts the young, committed teachers. Idealism, however, is only one of the criteria. Experience with minority children and desire to teach them are important. A practical, unsentimental approach is essential. We need teachers who are imaginative and practical, concerned, and objective. These are the ones we seek to hire.

However, many teachers have the ability to change and/or the ability to adjust. Supported by the school administration, aided by his or her colleagues, enlisting in the Intergroup Education Project's valuable offerings, the teacher can gain understanding—factual and pragmatic —of the culture which has shaped his students' attitudes toward learning. A teacher-education supervisor at the University who often speaks at our workshops, recently made a memorable statement to the teachers: "You must know yourself," he said. "You must have confidence in yourself, and you must be free of guilt about race."

Not a simple prescription, but truly a therapeutic one. Facing the fact of prejudice, erasing it as we work together, is the way. That, plus knowledge that gives understanding, is what the Intergroup Education Project has provided.

17

"Our Impatience Is of
The Highest Order"

I SHALL NEVER FORGET THAT DAY—August 23, 1963—
when the voice of Reverend Martin Luther King, Jr.,
rang out to the crowd of 500,000 who had joined the
March on Washington, proclaiming "Now is the time! Now
is the time to make real the promise of democracy."

Nor shall I forget the impassioned plea of Reverend
Hazaiah Williams, Negro board member, as Berkeley's
"Now is the time!" decision moved to fulfillment. "We
don't want anyone in this community to get the idea that
this board, 13 years after the Supreme Court decision to
desegregate our schools, is at all satisfied, or even patient,
with the progress we have made," said the Reverend Williams. "OUR IMPATIENCE IS OF THE HIGHEST
ORDER."

It had taken six years to bring the community to desegregate its secondary schools in 1964. Now, two years and
eight months later, we strove for a deadline date to desegregate our elementary schools, thus achieving total desegregation.

Gaining consensus was a stormy process. During an
intensive four weeks of board meetings and workshops,
from April 18 to May 16, 1967, we had to brace ourselves
to hold back our impatience. Our spirits went up and
down, as the community expressed itself for "integration
now" or "integration later," which might be never. Reluc-

tant parents who feared busing sent their most eloquent and prominent spokesmen. The whole array of reactionaries and racists who had tried to stop secondary integration in 1964 came out again in full force. I, for one, did not know if we were going to win.

The decision grew out of a series of dialogues, a series of pressures, and an intensive argument over the plan for integration. Step-by-step, the process fell into a pattern.

First, there was a movement for voluntary reverse busing, that is, busing white children to ghetto schools by parents who wished to do so. A striking finding in our evaluation of our token busing with federal funds, of 238 Negro children to white schools, had been the statement by 27 per cent of the Caucasian parents sampled in the receiving schools that they would favor busing their children down to the primarily Negro schools. We now estimated that approximately 100 white parents might be expected to volunteer to send their children.

Many Negro parents pressed for this move. They invited the white children, almost as if inviting them to a party, to come on the bus to share their schools which had been vastly improved during recent years by outstanding principals and federal funds. They urged them to come and mix with their children for the good of both races. Many called it, over and over again, "an act of faith" by the white parents in sharing the pioneer burden of desegregation busing which up to now they alone had shouldered.

However, not all white parents, even some of those most deeply committed to integration, were so sure the move would be a good one. Yes, it would be another wedge to crack the segregation pattern. It would be a personal demonstration of concern and commitment. But, without a plan for careful heterogeneous grouping, it could also create another segment of discrimination and isolation. If the Caucasian children were more advanced in achievement, which was generally the case, they would be set apart for learning at a higher level and the superiority stereotype and separation would again be reinforced. Furthermore, many white parents who were committed to total integration felt this would be a poor substitute. If the voluntary program were unsuccessful the long range goal of complete integration could be set backward.

It could be only a good-hearted but sentimental move. If it failed, it could be a step backward.

I was very doubtful, and I said so. Voluntary busing has not worked in any city where it has been tried. It has not worked in Oakland. It has not worked in Boston, where white children have mounted the bus bound for Negro schools "within the legal and moral traditions of the community,"* the community where Negro emancipation began. It is at best only an interim measure. However, perhaps it *would* work in Berkeley. We could give it a try, if the majority so decided.

At the April 18 (1967) board meeting I was asked to prepare a plan for volunteer reverse busing. However, the events of the meeting completely reversed the directive. That same night the Berkeley Federation of Teachers spoke for its carefully designed integration plan "More Effective Schools," and the Berkeley Teachers Association urged total integration by way of the citizen-staff elementary integration plan recommended and tabled in 1964. What's more, the Berkeley Teachers Association urged that its plan be implemented in September, 1967, five months later!

Then board member Samuel Schaaf asked for board commitment to "all deliberate speed." I objected to that much abused phrase although I knew the board member

* Robert Coles, *Integrated Education*, February-March, 1966.

had not suggested it as a means of inaction and delay. I suggested a deadline of September 1, 1968, for complete desegregation.

Then some leaders from the Negro community spoke up in a moving appeal for action:

> We're here to help each other. We don't have to be ashamed because we're poor. I was poor, of course—most of us here are.

> When I was very poor, I tried to get rich—I scrimped and saved to buy myself one expensive dress that everybody'd know where it came from, like Saks-Fifth Avenue. Now I'm not quite so poor—my kids are grown up and on their own. And I go and buy a dress at the cheapest store in Berkeley. I can do that now. *Now I know I can come up from West Berkeley and tell the school board what I want for my grandchildren and chances are I'll get it, no matter where I bought this dress.* What I want for my grandchildren is integration NOW!

> Many of us have been aware of the research which shows that compensatory education does not do all that is required. We want our children to learn to live with *all* the people *now.* As taxpayers, we have cooperated with the schools—we have supported its elections on bond issues and tax increases, we have voted for its fair-minded candidates. We have proved our concern for our schools and for our children. We want to implement total integration *now.*

Finally, toward midnight, another Negro mother stood up and said: "Let's stop pussyfooting around. We all know that total integration is what we've got to have. Let's get on the ball and *do* something. LET'S DO IT NOW!"

Then this mother: "Let's quit talking. I could say a lot. I just stammer here for words. But we all know what we're talking about. Let's shut up our mouths and do it!"

At last came the board resolution:

In entering a period of intensive discussion and decision with respect to the many different possibilities for achieving integration in the Berkeley schools, the Board wishes to affirm its general commitment to the principle of eliminating de facto segregation in the Berkeley School District, within the context of quality education, and aiming toward a date not later than September 1968.

But that was not the end. At the May 7 board meeting that followed, a huge crowd, some 650, showed up including many opponents. At the May 8 board workshop, strong opposition was again expressed. The board was beset by conflicting pressures—some to move the deadline up to September, 1967, some to abolish the deadline altogether.

Finally, on May 16, the action of April 18 was reaffirmed, and deadlines for completion of interim steps were assigned—October for the administrative recommendation on the specific plan, January or February of the next year for board decision on the plan.

The administrative staff worked all the summer that followed that meeting. The planning was difficult and complex. It had to be accomplished despite school housing deficiencies and with limited funds. We had to develop a transportation system for 3,500 of our almost 9,000 elementary pupils. All our educational programs had to be tailored to the change, for moving bodies alone would doom this undertaking to failure from the beginning. Schools and classes, schedules, grouping practices had to be reorganized. Special education, guidance, counseling, recreation, intergroup education must be related immediately to the changed system. Instructional materials and equipment must be revised and enhanced.

Teacher recruitment, selection, placement, in-service training must from the very beginning carry out the quality integrated education pattern. More Negro teachers must be recruited and at the board meeting we pledged ourselves to a major effort. The regular budget must be cut where possible to implement the needs of this priority. Supplementary funds—federal, state and local—must be continuously sought. Community, staff, and student involvement must be built into the whole process to an extent never reached before. Organized support must be comprehensive in the face of the insistent, hard-core opposition that remains.

We had to move fast but we had to move wisely. I am reminded of a timeless quote of Dr. Margaret Mead: "There is great advantage in moving fast if you move completely, if social, educational, and recreational changes keep pace. You must change the whole pattern at once and the whole group together—*and the people themselves must decide to move.*"

The people in Berkeley, black and white together, had made the decision.

18

Integration 1968: The Berkeley Plan

ON THE NIGHT OF JANUARY 16, 1968, the Berkeley Board of Education voted unanimously for a plan to desegregate its 14 elementary schools in September, 1968. The decade-long argument was ended, the decision made, the process begun.

If the leaders of any school district think school integration is an easy job, they had better not tackle it. Integration is difficult. But integration is also a wonderful, exciting, and therapeutic process—therapeutic both to the community and to every individual involved. If a community is open to this process, let its leaders follow Berkeley's path. Nothing is simple about the Berkeley plan, but it has worked.

The solution to segregation is as complex as the problem itself, with its built-in injustice and inequities. And so the plan to eliminate the problem in one area of our society cannot be simple. At first glance, the K-3, 4-6 plan, the Berkeley plan, sounds uncomplicated enough. The city is divided into four school attendance zones. Within those zones or strips running from lower Berkeley to the hills, the kindergarten through grade 3 children attend one of up to four schools in middle Berkeley or the hills; grades 4 through 6 attend one of four schools in South and West Berkeley. The walkers, according to state requirements, are the K-3 children living within three-fourths of a mile and the grades 4-6 children living within one mile of their schools, and safety provisions at crossings are made for them. Approximately 3,500 of the city's 9,000 elementary school children are bused. Pre-school children attending the various children's centers are bused in line with a board decision and the parents' request.

Within each zone the ratio of children will be balanced according to that of the total school population—50 per cent white, 41 per cent Negro, 9 per cent Oriental and other races. As far as possible this ratio will be followed in each school and each classroom, and a balance of socioeconomic backgrounds is maintained.

The significant difference between the Berkeley plan and other plans for integration of elementary schools is the two-way busing. Negro and white children are bused—Negro children ride up to mix with their white classmates in middle Berkeley and the hills in grades K-3, white children come down to mix with Negro classmates for the fourth through sixth grades. Berkeley is the only city I can cite that has thus equalized the burden of busing. The usual pattern has been to close a Negro school or two and bus the Negro children to white schools. This is saying, in effect, "It doesn't matter if we close your school," or "It isn't good enough to be used for integration." It is saying to the Negro children "*You* come to *us*." We decided on two-way busing because of its impartiality and because the middle and hill schools in Berkeley are the best physical plants for the young children, the lower Berkeley plants the best for the older ones. Under the K-3, 4-6 plan, virtually every elementary pupil in the city will share in the busing experience for approximately half of his elementary years.

To use our present school sites is also the only way we can do it *now*. Either we desegregate within existing plants or we wait for millions in federal funds to help build an educational park or two. We have studied developing educational parks in Berkeley, and some day we hope to build one. But we know that the funds we would need will not be forthcoming until the Viet Nam war ends and that mangled country is rebuilt—and until American cities begin to be rebuilt. We know the wait will be long when even the small amounts for Head Start have been whittled down. Integration cannot wait.

That is the physical, logistic part of the Berkeley plan. The educational part of the plan has been worked out even more intensively, and will be reworked as we proceed. It will be evaluated every step of the way and improved according to the findings. We have stated our educational goals as follows: "An integrated school environment that lessens prejudice and discrimination. Each class heterogeneous, reflecting the community's racial, socio-economic and intellectual diversity."

How will we reach these idealistic goals? By the means at hand—the skills of teachers (enhanced by special training), guidance staff, trained teacher-aides, parent aides; by tutoring by teachers, the School Resource Volunteers group (many of them university students), and by students tutoring students; by team-teaching and non-graded programs; by a flexible curriculum; by help from university specialists.

We hope to maintain the current pupil-teacher ratio of 26 to one. Primary grade classes will average about 24 children each. Grades 5-6 will have approximately 28 students per class.

Pupils will be grouped heterogeneously to avoid the old segregation through tracking in integrated classrooms. Groupings will be flexible, and individualized instruction in small groups will be emphasized. A running record of each pupil's progress in every subject area is kept as he moves from grade to grade, or school to school so that his teachers and his parents can follow the child's progress as well as his problem areas. Curriculum committees draft subject matter "continuums" that define the standards, the scope, and sequence to be followed in each area, so that teachers, pupils, and parents can see the over-all plan and can understand what is expected of each pupil at each level.

Tutoring, through all the means I have mentioned, helps personalize the classroom as well as providing extended remedial help. Teacher tutoring of parents may also be available.

A student center to serve children in crisis will be established in every school to provide the outside help a teacher needs to handle the individual and classroom relationship. A crisis situation can occur in any child's school experience. With major changes in their schools, tension and anxiety among children can be expected. An unsettled child may initiate an aggressive outburst that disrupts the classroom, a grief reaction, or withdrawal. Sending a child under stress to the principal's office or sending him home is not the answer. In the student center a special teacher, with teacher aides at hand, can provide a quiet setting and relief. Classroom activity can continue. The child may need to stay a few hours or a day or two, then he returns to his regular classroom.

The district's High Potential Program, which is more extensive than that supported by the state, will be expanded to include more gifted children by expansion of the criteria for selection. To academic performance will be added creative ability and creative potential as the teacher sees it in the student. Standard tests will be only one determining factor.

A learning laboratory, located in a separate room equipped with special materials and staffed by a teacher-specialist, will enable children to pursue individual projects. The teacher will guide the child in his activities, assist him in choosing materials and encourage him to experiment.

Now, how much does all this cost? Original estimates, made in the fall of 1967, set the over-all cost of elementary desegregation's first year (1968-1969 fiscal year) at $518,-138. This amount covered busing, learning laboratories, help centers, school plant and classroom remodeling, equipment relocation, and a variety of other items. The busing cost was estimated at $219,000, half of which is returned to the school district by the state, through Health, Education and Welfare Department funds. Thus the net cost to the district for busing is approximately $110,000, less than one-fourth of the total cost of the first year of integration. This cost is expected to remain substantially the same. The total cost of the desegregation program, however, is expected to decline to $302,460 for the 1969-1970 fiscal year and to $287,806 for the 1970-1971 fiscal year.

Since Berkeley's 1968-1969 school budget was set at approximately $19,371,616, the cost of elementary desegregation amounted to only 2.67 per cent of the total cost of school operation during that year. Berkeley's experience shows again that to integrate the community must contribute far more in efforts of the heart and will than in financial ways.

19

The Night of Decision: "We Drew a Circle Which Took Him In"

WHEN THE BOARD OF EDUCATION committed itself to total desegregation "no later than September 1968," I said that "Berkeley will make history at that time." Berkeley has made history, has begun to change history, may help America find a way to redeem post-Civil War history. Now on January 16, 1968, the board was ready to make its historic decision on an elementary integration plan. Almost exactly ten years ago—January 7, 1958—the NAACP first presented to the board the fact of de facto segregation in Berkeley schools.

We had had eight months to work it out. The community had been totally involved. Immediately after the board's April commitment to desegregation, we had broadcast by personal letters and press publicity an invitation to all agencies and individuals to submit plans. Some fifty plans and suggestions poured into the office of experts we set up to analyze the plans. Both teacher organizations evolved plans. Five were screened out and presented to the public for consideration. And finally, some 30 administrators and staff members worked day and night through five days in closeted sessions at a local hotel and came out with two plans to recommend. The K-3, 4-6 plan for integrated school zones was our primary recommendation.

Now that the long argument had ended the decision was to be made.

Let me tell you I sat uneasily on my chair at that board meeting. I looked out into an audience of some 1,200, recognizing many integration supporters, recognizing also old and new opposition groups, old and new enemies. Few, probably none, would be caught dead voicing outright bigotry.

I could pick out those who feared busing, those who clung to the neighborhood schools. They must not have heard our report at the board meeting of October 3, 1967, more than three months before. They must not have read the press articles about bus safety records, reported in our local paper, proving that children are safer on the bus than almost anywhere else. Each school day in the United States more than 16 million children are bused to school on more than 225,000 buses. The buses travel 1,800,000,000 miles annually, and yet according to the National Safety Council a school bus is 64 times safer than riding in the family car, five times safer than riding on any other kind of bus, four times safer than riding on a train, and twice as safe as flying on a scheduled commercial airliner. Even these statistics did not dispel some parents' fears and they came ready to fight the issue again.

There sat those parents who say "I'm for integration but I can't use my child to further my beliefs," and those who have said "We're for integration but let's wait until the Negro children are ready, till they've been educated up to *us* in good Negro schools." I knew too that there were many in the audience—in any audience facing an issue— who were neither pro nor con, who were waiting to hear what was decided. Then some of them would get on the band wagon, sharing the community limelight, and some would just string along. In the end almost everybody would want to share the winning side.

Most dangerous of all in the audience were those who would counsel delay. "We are for integration," they would say, "but let us wait and make a better plan." Some, voicing this, would be lying through their teeth; others—very few—would be sincere in their belief that a better plan could be made. But how well I know, as former board member Judge Avakian quoted later, that "Delay is the deadliest form of denial."

And we had made every effort to review all possible plans. If any more plans could have been distilled out of the community, if any further airing of the plans considered could have been provided, I do not know how it could have been done. The public was involved almost to the point of exhaustion.

That night in the Berkeley Community Theater I actually did not know what was going to happen. The board members do not tell *me* how they are going to vote! Four members I thought would vote Aye. I did not know about the fifth member, who earlier had suggested a teacher poll on the recommended K-3, 4-6 plan. How would he vote now? And I could not be certain that any one of the members might not be swayed by what would be said that night.

An Ad Hoc Committee had surfaced to demand, at the last minute, a secret poll of the community on the plan, claiming to have 3,000 signatures to its petition for such a poll. Its spokesmen were there in force and scheduled to speak. Several prominent citizens were counseling delay.

And Black Power *was* and *is* threatening. Berkeley is no island, immune to militant black power to the south in Oakland, to the north in Richmond and west across the Bay in San Francisco. Black Power grows in Berkeley—in the Black Student Union, the dignified Afro-American Society, the Black Muslims who seek to lead separate, superior Negro education, and the militant Black Panthers.

We were working to meet their legitimate demands, but work was slow. At the preceding meeting, January 3, the board had adopted a resolution pledging the district to attempt to hire Negro teachers in closer proportion to the number of Negro students. A tough promise to keep! At that time the Berkeley school system had 15 per cent Negro teachers and to get even that proportion we had recruited vigorously. Recall the pitifully small number of teachers our own state's teacher-training institutions turned out—25 Negroes graduated as teachers in 1967. Recently we had been scouring the southern states, sending recruiting teams to schools of education, Negro, and in some cases, integrated. The resolution directed me also to underline the district's commitment by an annual report of progress. Black Power was satisfied and silent at this meeting.

As I waited for the meeting to begin, I thought of a bomb threat or two, of the obscene red letters painted on the new white boat my sons and I had bought, of the poison-pen letters and threatening phone calls that poured into my office during the past months. Letters that asked questions or expressed honest worries, telephoners or visitors who did the same, were answered by my staff and me. We had announced in my weekly *Gazette* column that we welcomed calls and letters. We listened to those parents honestly disturbed, some of them wondering if they should move away. We sent them factual material. We thanked them for calling. There had been many, many calls.

How many will move? Everyone wondered. A local columnist claimed, "There is no escaping the possibility that many, if not all with small children, consider the school in selecting a neighborhood in which to buy and raise their family . . . Lots of parents want their little offspring close at hand, where they can get to the school easily, attend school affairs in the evening, and have kids that are their children's schoolmates as their playmates after school and over weekends. . . . And that, frankly, we

suspect is why a lot of fine Berkeley families are moving
out of the city. . . ."

But the predicted mass exodus after the secondary
schools were desegregated in 1964 failed to materialize. I
had to admit the difference, though, when the busing
affected little children. I did have the hope that if some did
leave Berkeley in search of a neighborhood school, others
would want to move in. A Berkeley real estate broker had
suggested this to me.

> The recent controversies regarding policies of the School
> Board move me to write you from the point of view of a real
> estate man handling numerous rentals in Berkeley. During
> the course of the last few months I have received many
> calls from people who specifically state they wish to move
> to Berkeley because they want their children to go to school
> in Berkeley. They are aware that they will pay a premium
> for living in Berkeley because of the current housing short-
> age. Some of these people specifically wish to have their
> children go to Berkeley schools because the Berkeley schools
> are in the process of being integrated, and these are white
> people not black who are calling me. It is my impression
> that the Berkeley School System is rapidly becoming famous
> for the high quality of its education and for its willingness
> to cope with the social problems of integration. Further-
> more, I feel that there are more people moving into Berkeley
> because of the improved school situation than are leaving
> Berkeley.

I felt better as I recalled that letter. All these thoughts
and feelings occupied me as I listened to the speakers on
the agenda. Fourteen speakers! And then, before the
board's vote on the plan, seven more were added.

Old stuff, I thought, half-listening for a while to the
opposition. Integration will downgrade rather than foster
academic excellence. . . . Busing some 3,500 students will
be dangerous and expensive. . . . Higher taxes will be

levied on property owners. . . . Support of the plan has political undertones. That last one irked me especially. Political undertones? What support, what opposition has not? Who is not political? What is community change if not a political process? I measured the applause as these speakers ended their opinions and threats. Some of it frightened me.

The head of the Ad Hoc Committee, which that night claimed 2,800 signers to its petition for a secret citizen poll, got considerable applause after he challenged the wisdom of the plan. Would he win that poll if the board voted for delay? I was forced to challenge him when he charged that 25 per cent of the sixth-grade students in West Berkeley cannot read. "It's ridiculous for an intelligent man to make such a statement," I said. Then board member Carol Sibley stood up beside me and refuted the charge by reading the statistics in the School Master Plan Committee report. Now our side got the applause.

We would have received even more if we had had the report of State Assemblyman Leroy F. Greene, released in the press five weeks later, of results of reading and intelligence tests in every California school district with at least 1,000 students. Of 29 East Bay districts included, 14 were far above the statewide average. The poorest results were in districts with numerous children from minority groups —*except in Berkeley.* The minority group pattern was broken by the Berkeley schools, with scores significantly above average. Berkeley and San Francisco have about the same percentage of minority students, Greene pointed out, yet Berkeley scores were 58, 67, 57, and 58 as compared to San Francisco's 41, 36, 40, and 38 (50 is the median).

Applause swelled again when former board member Judge Spurgeon Avakian, veteran pioneer for school integration, took the mike and said, "Boards of Education are elected to make policy, not to conduct polls," and again when Marc Monheimer, chairman of the School Master Plan Committee, declared, "The case for integration is basically a legal and a moral one, not a scientific one. We must integrate *now*, not simply because Negro achievement is helped, but because our survival depends on it. If we are to endure as a nation, or as a city, we cannot produce another generation of white bigots."

So the meeting went, up and down, opponents and supporters interspersed, demanding to "Wait," urging to "Do it NOW." My spirits went up and down accordingly. What would the board decide? As the long meeting moved to its climax I thought I felt a groundswell of affirmation, the tide of victory rising. I sensed the process of persuasion, the kind of "If you can't lick 'em, join 'em" change, the need for community solidarity and to be on the winning side.

Finally the vote approached—the long procession of 21 speakers had come to an end. Several board members rose to express, in a few words, their conviction. Sam Schaaf said, "I think we should decide on it and turn our efforts . . . to the much more important question of improvements in our educational program. We have a historic opportunity." The Reverend Hazaiah Williams spoke with his usual eloquence. David Nelson spoke last. His earlier call for a poll had been misinterpreted, he said. Now that the teachers' organizations, which have worked so intensively on the plan, are satisfied, he is satisfied. "I feel we should act tonight," he declared. "I believe there are great advantages to this plan and that it is well thought out."

And now the vote. Tom Wogaman, my special assistant, called the roll as usual. Only this roll call was dramatic—one could sense the emotion in the atmosphere. Alphabetically, Tom called out the names—first, "Director Nelson?", and Nelson's quiet "Yes!"; "Director Grosberg?,"

"Yes!"; Director Schaaf?", "Yes!", "Director Sibley?", "Yes!", and "Director Williams?" with his resounding "Aye!"

Victory! Unanimity! Now the audience rose in a body and applauded, a crowd came up to shake our hands and embrace us, and we dispersed to various homes to celebrate.

20

The Berkeley Plan: Designed to Succeed

WE COULD ENJOY the growing community feeling of accomplishment in Berkeley as the press and television, local and national, reported our victory. We could hope that even the dissidents might share the glow. But we could not long indulge our satisfaction. The plan must be successful. It cannot fail. Too much is at stake.

I do not say that success will come overnight or in one year. Time is needed to work with the staff to develop the new philosophy—the new philosophy that should be old— that should have come into fruition long ago. Time is needed to work out proper approaches for handling children in heterogeneous groups.

The remaining core of dissident elders will plague us and attempt to slow us. If a roof leaks, they will say we cannot afford to keep our roofs intact because we are pouring all the money into integration. If there are not enough pencils handy, some staff member will make a careless remark that we cannot afford pencils and integration both. If a window is broken, they'll blame the Negro kids whom they think "should have stayed down there where they belong." They will continue to gun for us on busing, our primary extra cost. Yet this cost, half of which is covered by the state, is only about one per cent of our budget.

But in spite of the minor grumblings within our midst, in spite of the reaction that surrounds us, in spite of growing Black Power, integration will survive and grow in Berkeley. Berkeley has won its quiet revolution. We shall not turn back. Whether or not we can change adults, we *can* change children. Our children will grow up in a community where justice is a way of life, and, we hope, they will spread justice. As President Kennedy said, "We have the power to make this the best generation of mankind in the history of the world, or to make it the last."

Our planning began on a broad scale in April, 1967, when the board had committed the district to "integration no later than September, 1968." When, in January, 1968, the board voted to implement the K-3, 4-6 plan, specific and widespread action started. Everyone involved with the schools, and everyone who wants to be involved with them, was given an opportunity to share the integration process. Teachers, administrators, school staff members from classroom to office desk, PTA's, religious leaders, city officials, housewives, businessmen, service clubs and public agencies, parents and grandparents and uncles and aunts, and most important of all, the students themselves, got into the act.

Throughout the spring of 1968, adults and children of all races rode up and down the hills to talk, to listen, to eat and play together in the interests of integration. Truly, Berkeley became a different city, mixed and melded together by a common aim and a mutual process.

I cannot begin to list all the activities during that spring. We do not even know what everyone has done because some of the most significant efforts have been made in the privacy of individual consciences. Consider this letter sent to me by one set of Berkeley parents: "Not long ago we opposed busing for reasons which were both abstract and selfish. We now acknowledge the fact that personal compromises are necessary to build a healthy community. We prefer that our children grow up loving and aware rather than protected, secure and isolated." I believe many Berkeley parents reached a breakthrough that spring in many small house meetings, where they could candidly air their hopes, fears, insights and misconceptions and join with courage and commitment our plan for integration.

When the Intergroup Education Project asked for a pledge to work for integration, hundreds of responses poured in. This was the pledge they had mailed out:

> I have a personal commitment to integration. I am willing to involve two or three others or more in some meaningful way.
>
> I do not plan to say, 'Let George do it,' now when time may be running out for meaningful dialogue between groups.

And when Intergroup sent out a letter suggesting house meetings on integration and the integration plan, 240 housewives responded, including some offers from housewives in our nearby all-white suburban cities.

The almost overwhelming response of support was beyond our strongest hopes. It cheered us as we worked, from early breakfast meetings to meetings far into the night, to firm up the plan.

Let me just outline the process that led up to Integration 1968. We set up an Office for Elementary Integration, to coordinate the efforts of district personnel and community agencies and individuals as well as to serve as a public information center. This office had ultimate responsibility for school site preparation, busing, street-crossing safety for children walking to school, heterogeneous attendance according to school population, library services, community involvement, Elementary and Secondary Education Act aid, evaluation, publications, instructional materials, data processing, and business services. It operated a speakers' bureau, organized and coordinated zone meetings and school exchanges within the zones. The office planned and directed a teacher exchange program through which every teacher spent a week in a school different racially from his or her regular school.

Meanwhile some principals were reassigned, according to their skills and desires. Teachers too sent in their preferences for school assignment. Some could work better with the younger children, some with the older; some had specialities they could use more valuably with one age level than the other.

The human logistics were a massive undertaking. In assigning pupils, we sought to establish a comprehensive spread in all areas—behavior, age, emotional development, achievement, ability—but the primary requirement was that the student population pattern be maintained with 50 per cent white, 41 per cent Negro, 9 per cent other. We wanted each classroom to contain good models of behavior, work habits, achievement and creativity so that each child might have a comfortable role to play among his peers. Exceptions to the rule of attending school in zone of residence had to be cleared. The regular exceptions— health, extended day care, private child care, pupil adjustment (guidance and special education cases)—could be quickly handled. But there were other requests for exceptions by parents whose children wanted or needed to stay with classmates. (In most cases, zone by zone, children *were* being moved with classmates.) Among these requests were those from some of the parents of the 238-250 Negro children who had been bused to white schools by the ESEA project. The board adopted a policy of flexibility within the framework of the stated heterogeneous pattern. All of this demanded a lot of work in juggling data.

We had a computer helping us all along the way. On the last day of school, the last day of segregation, every parent was sent a card stating where his child would go to school (this, of course, was in the main implicit in each zone), what classroom, and the bus routes. The card also informed the parents that in late August they would be told the bus stop their child would use. This again was a complex task, especially in Berkeley's hills where circuitous roads are at places impossible for use by school buses. Cards for all students in their classrooms were given to the teachers who could become acquainted with the background and needs of each of their students.

The physical plants presented many obstacles to change. At a meeting the day after the board voted to desegregate, three hours were taken up just listing the jobs to be done—making some rooms larger, some smaller, changing toilets to kindergarten size, reviewing fire protection, remodeling playgrounds, moving desks, blackboards, chairs, electronic equipment, and more.

Meanwhile the educational plan was being worked and reworked throughout the summer. Now heterogeneity is a great word, but to bring it into action takes all the innovative skill teachers and specialists can summon. The seeds of tracking could not be planted in our hard-won integration plan. Consider reading, for instance. In the primary grades there would be children reading above grade level, and there would be minority children below grade level. The reading class must be racially mixed, yet individual needs must be filled. The high group could be mostly white, the low group mostly black. How do you handle this situation?

Throughout the spring teachers met in intensive workshops on reading. They reviewed all the programs in use —I think there were nine at that time. I had emphasized reading above all other subjects and although some principals had favorite programs each teacher was free to use the one she thought best for the children and with which she felt most comfortable. We knew no teacher would go back to the fundamentalist systems of the good old days. Actually, we had a rich fund of programs, including a "homemade" one at Columbus school designed by the teachers and staff. Under the direction of a University of California reading specialist, the teachers' workshop devised still another program. The key is that all children, whether fast or slow in learning, can work together in one group while they grasp the basic idea of the words of a story or text. They get it as newspaper readers catch a good headline. Then the concept is broken down and adapted to the varying learning levels while children work in smaller groups.

"You can teach anything to anybody if he gets the basic idea," the specialist says. "You make it simple so all can understand, then develop it according to the children's pace and ability." Putting this program into action, she told us, has never been done before.

Many other activities that prepared for integration, I am sure, have never been done before. And I am absolutely certain so *much* has never been done before in any school community. The new school zones steamed with activity. One open house after another brought Negro parents up the hill, white parents down the hill—to schools and to homes. The schools in the Negro community brought out 500 to 1,500 in attendance. Persons of all races opened up their homes to meetings. Special school events were staged for the children who would be together in September. There were interracial ball games, picnics, barbecues.

Our Intergroup Education Project led the way. During a series of fortnights of offerings for the teaching staff, volunteer teachers offered 39 demonstrations of means and methods for integration. I wish I could list them all. They ranged from "Science as Related to Race" to "How to Handle Name-Calling." They included a dialogue between Black Student Union leaders and teachers, and all their efforts added up to a package that would revolutionize any interracial community.

One project centered around me. An Intergroup Youth Council was formed, 50 children, 2 or 3 third to fifth-graders from each school, were selected by their classmates as members. The council met at the Administration Building once a month for a whole morning. Part of the morning was entertainment, part questions and answers, which is where I came in, at 11 o'clock. They would sing "Integration Calypso."

> Sing a little song of integration
> Berkeley will be watched by the whole nation
> When you and I make a date
> To integrate . . . in sixty-eight.

> In 1954 the Supreme Court said
> School segregation should be dead
> So Berkeley is about to lead the way
> To integrated schools and a bright new day.

> The color of our skin is no big deal
> We all have feelings that are real
> And we expect that with integration
> We'll have equal quality education.

> School people are working day and night
> To make sure everything will be done just right
> The hopes of the future rest on us
> And all the little children riding in the bus.

One day I came in as they were playing the "circle game." The children stood in a circle, hand in hand, black and white and Oriental all mixed up. They were repeating these words,

> They drew a circle which
> kept him out.
>
> But love and I had the wit
> to win.
>
> We drew a circle which
> took him in.

Then the children formed a large circle around me and got down to the nitty-gritty. They asked me questions, and they talked back and forth as I listened. I asked them what they are thinking about next fall.

"Everybody thinks there'll be a lot of fights," said a Negro girl.

"Aw, white kids get into fights too," answered a white boy.

"Some white kids don't like to make friends with black kids," one Negro girl remarked and up went a flock of hands in protest.

"That's only a rumor," said the first one with her hand up. "White kids aren't all just one kind any more than Negro kids are."

Then a tiny girl with big blue eyes stood up and said: "Well, it really doesn't matter about the color of skin. You should treat others as you would treat any member of your family."

By the time the school year's last and fourth meeting of the council came around, I saw that these 50 children, white and black, felt that they were pioneers, that they would lead the way through the woods of prejudice.

Intergroup has led the socializing as well as the soul-searching. They even organized what they call "little things." These little things include a sewing group (inter-racial), making dresses for children who need them, children's garden clubs to help beautify the city, and collection of paperbacks to provide a personal library for every child in Berkeley who has not started one.

Little things—big things—you name it, we're doing them.

21

Unfinished Business:
Secondary School Integration

THERE ARE NO GAINS WITHOUT PAINS, as Adlai Steven-son used to say. Gains in school integration will be made with pains. In Berkeley, our exhilarating and widely supported process of preparation for total integration in September, 1968, suffered grievous wounds in April. While unanimity for elementary integration had grown, trouble had smoldered in the secondary schools, desegregated since September, 1964. Garfield Junior High School was the main center of potential trouble as I have written. Although much progress had been made, many fine interracial re-lationships established, and leadership by black and white together growing, troubles festered. Throughout the spring, one incident after another sent me to Garfield to calm things down and to return to work with my administrative staff on Garfield's problems. Then the principal, a dedicated and able man, resigned. He wrote, in part, in a letter to his colleagues:

> I believe we are confronted with significant numbers of par-ents and school personnel of all races who do not understand the concept of integration. Extremists exist in black and white who either intentionally or innocently could scuttle Berkeley's educational and social goals. . . . Challenges on rational grounds is constructive, but indiscriminate chal-lenge to school authority is dangerously destructive. The negative attitude of the parent is often reflected in the be-

havior of the student, and the student's chances of success diminish.

The death of Martin Luther King, Jr., in April ignited the frustration and anger of the Garfield black students into acts of violence and created an atmosphere of chaos. With the help of the high school's Black Student Union leaders we quelled the trouble. But damage had been done.

The *Berkeley Daily Gazette* compounded the damaging effects. The Garfield report was, of course, on page one, where it belonged. What did not belong there was the large headline "RACIAL FLARE-UP AT SCHOOL HERE." Under that, "STUDENTS REPORT BEATINGS." Along with reporting the events of the days after the assassination, the newspaper detailed incidents, mostly by black students, of violence or insult, that had happened throughout the school year. The newspaper got its information from a study of the problems of teachers' hall duty made by the California Teachers Association that had been leaked to the *Gazette* by a small, vitriolic right-wing group. To scream it at that explosive time, when violence was in the air, was in my opinion totally irresponsible. Berkeleyans now connected these age-old problems of discipline to integration. It was not only Garfield that was the target, but integration in general.

We had to cool the situation. We held meetings morning, afternoon, and night through the days that followed— meetings with parents, students, and students and parents together. Together we faced the situation with candor and together we planned constructive measures.

Meanwhile letters attacking integration and us, the integration leaders, poured into the *Gazette*. The paper provided an extra page to contain them. It even opened its letter column to letters without signature or address. They blasted us. And some of our supporters blasted back. Opponents threatened to move, and I'm sure some did move over the hill to the all-white communities where they would augment their resistance to change.

But equilibrium returned. At the board meeting of May 21, principals reported discipline problems under control, and at the board president's request I reported on behavior in the secondary schools.

I called Judge Spurgeon Avakian's words to the attention of the board: "You are the protectors of change, not the protectors of the status quo. The goal is not just community peace, the goal is education." I pointed out that we have a handful of troublemakers and we will always have troublemakers. I said all our problems will not be solved when desegregation becomes total in September, but we shall move ahead. I stressed the fact that today's young people, seeing the inequities in our society, the Viet Nam war, the Poor People's March on Washington, want and must have a voice, must be allowed to participate in change.

That night we *produced* change. The board voted to encourage heterogeneous grouping and eliminate tracking in secondary schools. As I have reported, we took the following interim steps: elimination of ability grouping for junior high school social studies, reduction of the number of tracks from four to three, and approval of open enrollment beginning in February, 1969, whereby students and their parents will have the prerogative of selecting a higher track. More than 400 students chose to take the upward step. Furthermore a staff task group was authorized to work during the summer to develop plans for a transition to a more heterogeneous method of grouping.

In March, 1968, I appointed a committee to study tensions in the secondary schools. I called it the Committee on Staff-Student Relations, Secondary Schools. Jeff Tudisco, chairman of the history department at Berkeley High School acted as chairman of the committee which became

known as The Tudisco Committee. I charged the committee to discover the causes of growing tensions among students; discover the causes of increasing alienation between
students and staff; offer solutions to these problems.

The committee of 12—a psychologist, a counselor, two
vice-principals, one principal, one coordinator of special
programs and five teachers representing each major subject area—interviewed students, staff, and parents. It also
distributed questionnaires to the entire school staff. Its
conclusions, in sum, were these:

> *The overall Berkeley public school (secondary) envi-
> ronment creates hostility and alienation, especially among
> minority students. It is not conducive to the most basic,
> human forms of communication.* Misunderstanding, tension,
> hostility exist not only between various elements of the stu-
> dent body but between students and faculty as well. The
> blame for these conditions rests upon the adults in the
> schools who have inherited and fostered the system. More
> regulations and more persons functioning in a police capac-
> ity will not solve our problems.

The committee made 82 recommendations for change!
Recommendations for change and/or improvement were
made in the areas of staff effectiveness, curriculum, scheduling, tracking, personnel policies, student and community
involvement, extra curricular activities, and student welfare.

The Tudisco report on tensions was summarized and
circulated throughout the community. Its findings and recommendations were passed on to a Summer Task Force,
which worked all summer and reported its recommendations in September. Its report was distributed to all secondary staff; district-wide meetings were held so that
teachers and administrators could react: and student response was elicited. Then all reactions were synthesized
onto charts for study by a final Committee on Secondary

School Reorganization, which made specific recommendations to the board in February, 1969. By the time this book is published, the Berkeley secondary schools should be a model of another "quiet revolution."

I shall not burden the reader with the original 82 recommendations, nor with the lesser number finally presented to the board. I shall hit only the high spots. Let me point out here the areas that may be termed crucial.

Actively encourage teachers who are not agreeable to the District's integration policy to seek other employment.

Support administrators, up to and including court action, in the dismissal of staff members who ignore District philosophy and policy.

Inservice Training (for credit)

Implement immediately a mandatory inservice training program which includes a variety of choices for the participants and which focuses on growth in self-awareness and understanding in human relations.

The "variety" means a range of self-exploratory sessions that can be rugged "encounters" or small, less vigorous, home meetings. A grant to support this program has already been received.

Staff Utilization

Take action to make teaching assignments equitable, particularly those of a supervisory, non-teaching nature. Direct the principal of each school to form a committee of teachers for the purpose of assessing the matter of teaching duties and work load.

Assign reading consultants in English and history classrooms for informal, individual diagnosis of the reading needs of students. . . . Provide the services of reading consultants to the classroom teacher, allowing for reading to become a part of the entire curriculum.

Require that each secondary principal. . . . meet regularly with student groups, with curriculum associates, department heads and faculty, evaluate and supervise certificated staff, meet regularly with community groups, working through the office of the Director of Human Relations.

Allow counselors to start with students in Grade 9 and stay with the same students through Grade 12.

Create the position of Ombudsman. . . . to represent students.

Personnel Recruitment

Take full advantage of Berkeley's unique position to screen carefully from a large selection of student teachers.

Accept more teachers on a part-time basis to take advantage of the many talented people in this community who prefer not to work full time.

The philosophy expressed for curriculum development was this:

The potential that can be achieved in the growth of the individual student through exposure to creative and enlightening curriculum content has not been sufficiently tapped. Our goals for curriculum should be consonant with this high potential. A vital and relevant curriculum can engender in the student an appreciation for his unique and individual abilities and performances. It can stimulate changes in behavior. It can bring into meaningful relationship the two sets of experiences of the student—those occurring in school and in the world around him.

Inventive and creative curriculum should develop the student's potential for feeling and understanding as well as thinking and reasoning. It should build on the student's ability to reflect, analyze, observe, deduce and devise independent decisions and viewpoints.

There were recommendations concerning various means of grading, stressing the "pass/not pass" procedure.

Heterogeneous grouping was spelled out. Flexible scheduling was urged.

In sum, the report asked for a revolution to bring about educational democracy through basic and succinct changes.

A lot of action came out of these recommendations and the widely circulated Tudisco report from which they developed. Student leaders had responded vigorously to the report's findings. The Black Student Union had presented a list of 14 demands to the board, ranging from firing "racist" teachers to including "soul food" in the high school cafeteria. The board did not start firing teachers labeled "racist" by the students but restated the district's hiring policy of determining the applicant's lack of prejudice and commitment to integration. As for soul food, some of the most popular items were put on the cafeteria menu.

A comprehensive black studies program went into effect at Berkeley High School in February, 1969. It encompassed black history, African civilization, black economics, black literature, black journalism, African dance, Swahili, and the history of jazz. Black history and the history of jazz were already a part of the high school curriculum. Elements of all these areas were included in junior high schools as well—some in separate courses, some under social studies. At the high school the black studies courses were taught by black teachers. Most of the courses, even the difficult Swahili, drew a considerable number of both white and black students.

An experimental "community high school," a school-within-a-school, was initiated. The 116 students who enrolled attend regular classes the first four periods of the day, then the rest of the day, from 10:30 a.m. to 3 p.m. are free to plan and carry out their own educational projects. Off-campus research and on-campus discussion is based on material relating to English, history, science, art, drama,

dance, music, and physical education. Observation and research must be organized, then interpreted through a
report, an essay or poem, a painting, or even a dance.
Evaluation of what the student has accomplished follows.
The Community High School students are a mixture of
races, interests and achievement levels, diversity being a
major base for the experiment. Jay Manley, the drama in-
structor who initiated and developed the experimental
school, is finding it highly valuable in helping students
understand themselves, their relation to society as a whole
and their potential contribution. He sees it as pointing the
way to the high school of the future.

The ombudsman recommendation was activated in all
secondary schools and the teacher selected for this role
found himself busy listening to and adjusting students' and
teachers' grievances as well as their suggestions for
change.

Teacher training, especially in relation to the integrated classroom, was intensified. A 16-week in-service
program in Minority History and Culture began with 250
staff members and all teachers will eventually participate. Its two-part program includes "Historical Aspects"
and "Social Analysis" of the effects of individual and insti-
tutional racism. Oscar Brown, Jr., folksinger, poet, and
composer, opened the program. Other sessions included
lectures, discussions, debates, drama, panels, and films.
Teachers were led to react in one of three ways: through
participation in seminars, production of dramatic or visual
presentations, or participation in "sensitivity" or "encoun-
ter" group sessions. They chose the way they found most
comfortable.

At the junior high schools and ninth-grade West Campus there was a trend toward abandoning study halls as a
waste of time. At the students' suggestion the schools allowed students to decide how to use this time and per-

mitted them to leave the school grounds if they wished.

These were among the results of the Tudisco "tensions" report and the board's action on its recommendations. My successor, Dr. Foster, is opening more doors between teachers and students, schools and community. When a new principal was to be selected for Berkeley High School, on the retirement of its principal, he suggested and the board approved an advisory committee including not only district staff but also students and community laymen. He wants the students' judgment as to how the new principal relates to them as well as their "decision-influencing" power. He is also extending this decision-influencing to representatives of community groups.

Berkeley's "hot" spring in our desegregated secondary schools came to a close and we moved coolly ahead with elementary integration. I had to withdraw my caution, "One step at a time." We must build elementary integration from the beginning, and we must uproot the tensions in the desegregated but far from integrated secondary schools. We must rebuild their inner structure to fit the needs of contemporary students. Let me repeat Dr. Margaret Mead's statement that "the people themselves must decide to move." Integration does not come by magic. It comes by commitment, courage, by compromise and consensus, by facing trouble and learning thereby, by building and rebuilding, by hard work. The people in Berkeley, black and white, had moved as far as community consensus would permit when they desegregated the secondary schools in 1964. True they had begun at the wrong end, but better to begin there than not at all. Now, with renewed courage, Berkeley begins again—to rebuild secondary desegregation into a reality and to build anew, for the as yet disillusioned young, on a firm and sound foundation.

The End—And the Beginning

TUESDAY, SEPTEMBER 10, was "D Day" for Berkeley's "Integration '68." Would it also be our "V Day"? Would our buses roll to victory?

During the preceding week, I could scarcely sleep at night. Busy days of teacher orientation, long evenings of work to untangle last minute snarls; late registrations of students who must be fitted into our 41 per cent black, 50 per cent white, 9 per cent Oriental and other groups, heterogeneous classrooms; and then hours of worry lest, in spite of all our preparation, something should go wrong. I had no time to slip off to the Y for a relaxing swim, no time for weekend sailing. Although the planning and preparation had been a massive collective effort, the responsibility was mine—the responsibility for the safe busing of approximately 3,500 children and the safe walking of more than 5,000 others to schools ¾ to 1 mile from their homes, for the almost precise numerical classroom integration, *and* for the maintenance and improvement of quality education for which the district is known.

That week was historic in Berkeley in more fields than school integration. Black militants were threatening to "blow the town" if a guilty verdict was returned against Black Panther leader Huey Newton, who was accused of killing an Oakland police officer. Charges of unnecessary police force in quelling disorders were being made at overflow city council meetings that went on day and night. Telegraph Avenue and surrounding streets and borders of the UC campus were strewn with glass and plaster. Boarded-up windows replaced broken glass on streets silent and empty except for police patrols during the curfew hours. Days were stormy with mass meetings at which activists, students, and hippies sought a response to what they termed a police takeover.

On Sunday, September 8, the jury found Newton guilty of manslaughter. On Monday, the city lifted its "state of disaster." Monday was California's Admission Day, a holiday, but hardly a festive one. How would it be on our historic integration Tuesday? Would we keep our cool?

In effect, we certainly did keep our cool. But we were warm with excitement, exhilaration, and obvious success. Tuesday dawned sunny and beautiful. I was up at the crack of dawn, as were my young neighbors—all of us so eager for the day to begin, for the buses to begin to roll, that we could hardly wait. The kids teetered on their toes as they waited for the yellow buses to arrive at their pickup points. Each bus bore a number and the names of the schools it moved to and from as well as a picture of an animal—an elephant, giraffe, bear cub, or other—symbolizing the school for the young ones who could not yet read.

At 7:30 a.m. the buses began to roll from the transportation yard and soon the city was criss-crossed by the yellow buses. What a picture it would have made from a helicopter flying above as the buses skittered across town, up and down the hills, and around the wooded curves; many groups of children, waiting impatiently, parents trying to calm them down, and clusters of press photographers and television crews. That first day we bent the rules and let a few insistent parents ride. We also let one writer ride each bus.

At last—which was the way it seemed to us impatient ones—the buses arrived at the designated stops. The children in grades 4, 5, and 6, primarily white middle and upper-middle class, rode down from the hills to the four ghetto schools, formerly almost totally black. The young black children, kindergarten through grade 3, rode up from the ghetto to the formerly primarily white hill schools.

I rode with both groups—down from my hill with the older white children, back up with the crop of little black ones. Then I drove my car to another bus stop to ride another bus. The drivers, carefully selected from among many applicants, turned out to be mostly black—and mostly women. They were happy to have been chosen. True, more women applied, but also more women passed the rigid local and state tests. Those I saw and heard about were warm, motherly, and firm. In many cases some of their progeny were passengers and their mothers required them to be model riders. An aide rode along with the driver of every bus. In many cases the aide was a University of California student, helping earn her way through school.

My first driver was a large woman of 50 or so, who told me she was the oldest of 10 children and now is mother of six and grandmother of 15. Her aide was a white UC student, married, and like her husband, helping earn her way through school. Both were great with their young passengers—warm, friendly, and reassuring, but also firm. On one bus two boys in the back fooled around with a broom, moving in and out of their seats. When they got to their school, the bus driver quietly asked them to stay in their seats and, after the other students left, she went back and told them the rules in no uncertain terms. If they didn't sit quietly with their backs against the seat and feet on the floor, they might get thrown and hurt, she said. More than that, they might not be allowed to ride the bus. That settled them! One newcomer, a black child who had just moved to Berkeley, was very shy and frightened. She was reassured by her two seatmates and, at journey's end, each took her hand and, at the aide's direction, escorted her to the school office and gave her into the care of a parent volunteer.

But these were exceptions. As I have long known—ever since my first experience in busing rural children to town schools in New England—kids love the bus. It's the best part of the day because they're "going somewhere." They will be lively but they will also "behave."

There was an ebullience in the air. True, there were a few mishaps. It would have been amazing if there were not, in the complicated business of busing 3,500 children through a hilly, circuitous city. One bus took its load to the wrong school, but fortunately the mistake was discovered before the children entered the building. One bus stalled, although it was a new one. But by the time another bus arrived to take its place, the original bus was on its way again. In every case, transportation staff members and volunteers stood ready at their telephones and trailed the buses in their personal cars to help in case of first day trouble. Bill Rhodes, who had charge of the planning of the whole intricate business, drove around in his camper. A number of extra runs had to be made to accommodate children who, for one reason or another, had not made the bus. Again the staff was ready.

Some parents drove their children that first day, which only complicated the situation, since we needed to know just how the bus loads turned out. These personal drivers were mainly white parents. The black parents, even though theirs were the younger children who were being bused, had supported the busing from the start. Nevertheless, I was interested to see one young black man, hair styled high in African manner, transporting a load which included a young brother. As he let them out, he gave the Black Panther salute. The kids laughed merrily. They were not yet panthers—more like puppydogs.

At the schools many volunteers were on hand to help the staff welcome the children and guide them to their classrooms. In some schools, teachers on leave had come back to share the duties of integration's first day. One principal who invited six teachers on leave for imminent childbirth to help at his school was a bit worried lest his school population suddenly increase.

Parent volunteers came to act as hosts to the children, helped sort them out and take them by the hand to their new classrooms. Children who were old timers in their schools acted as hosts to the newcomers. This was particularly interesting in the four grades 4-6 schools in the ghetto, where black children were the ones to welcome their white classmates.

At 11 o'clock that morning I held a press conference, attended by a large crowd of reporters, radio and television staff, and several magazine writers. I was happy to report that every public school boy and girl in Berkeley was now enrolled in a desegregated classroom. I declared that it had gone beautifully, beyond our most optimistic expectations. This was a fact. "Beautiful" was the word I had heard from everyone—principals, teachers, parents, visitors.

Congratulatory wires had poured in, among them messages from Dr. Harold Howe, United States Commissioner of Education, Washington, D.C.; Mr. Roy Wilkins, Executive Director, N.A.A.C.P., New York; Mr. P. D. Haughton, Philco Ford Headquarters, Philadelphia, Pa.; Dr. Theron Johnson, United States Office of Education, Washington, D.C.; Mr. Whitney M. Young, Executive Director, National Urban League, N.Y. I was glad to read these to the press, hoping thus to underscore to the nation the conviction that integration *can* and *must* be accomplished. We also were visited that day by distinguished educational leaders from our state capitol and from other school districts.

Well, we all sighed with relief when that first crucial day was over. So far as we know, every child got home as safely and happily as he had bused to school that morning. Two disturbed mothers did call us, however. One mother was upset because her son had not come home at the time expected, but she called back to say she had just recalled that by arrangement her daughter had taken him to the dentist. And another phoned her concern, only to discover that her missing son was in the bathroom.

A great day! You could sense the exhilaration throughout the city. Where was this dread of busing, this great specter of fear? Vanished into the clear September air of that beautiful first day.

Busing in other communities has been used as the symbol of resistance to integration. Berkeley had been wise enough to understand this, brave enough to put its children on the bus.

Now the job at the end of the bus ride begins. So far I can say it is going well and I have no reason to believe it will not continue to go well and grow better and better. I believe Berkeley will be so accustomed to integrated elementary schools that it will soon seem that the schools have always been that way. During the first months of integration I visited the schools very frequently and asked for continual reports of all that went on.

I shall report the good side first. At the kindergarten through grade three schools, black-white relationships are very reassuring. Kindergarten children are practically colorblind. They have a playful curiosity about differences —and that's all. One sees a black child stroking the blonde hair of a white child lovingly, and a white child as interested in the beribboned pigtails or natural kinkiness of her black companion.

In the grades 4-6 schools, an advantage grows out of the fact that the white children come to the ghetto schools which the black children have been attending right along and near which many of them live. This was not the basis for the plan—rather the plan was chosen because the plants were larger and more suitable for the older students. But the black children now had the opportunity to be hosts to the new children on their home ground. Many of them happily took on this role. Although the white newcomers had visited the black schools during the year of preparation, their black classmates could now make them feel at home. For both groups it was a process of discovery.

In the grades 4-6 schools, children are pairing off, black and white, consciously because, during our intensive year of preparation, they came to understand what integration requires. They are interested in differences as they also find similarities and identification with one another. I watched pair after pair of these new-made friends playing happily together—the girls hand in hand, the boys jostling one another in usual kid fashion. They learn from one another's special skills. I learned that many of these children play together at their homes after school, sometimes in a black home, sometimes in a white one.

In the classroom I witnessed the same process of exchange.

There have also been some incidents—some pushing and shoving and hitting, lunch money thefts, some ostracism—a black child shut out of a white group, or a white child by a black group. These incidents have been quietly handled. They diminish, month by month. I was a barometer because I heard about them all—I heard them over the telephone and then I saw them in exaggerated form in the usual pile of hate mail. I trust the principals and counselors to handle trouble wisely, and if they need my help they know they can count on my coming.

I want to tell you now about this year's first meeting of the Intergroup Youth Council, 68 students from the four grades 4-6 schools who plan to meet monthly with the superintendent, as they did in 1967, to talk over problems and progress. These kids gave more insight into what goes on than any other source. As we sit in a big circle, they do most of the talking. Their role, they told me, is "to make friends," "to settle fights and arguments," "to get kids together—especially the lonesome ones," and "to get everybody to belong to something." They reported "fewer fights," "better relations," "more clubs and activities." One white boy said some bright students get bored and get less attention than they're used to because the "less bright" students need so much help. My answer was they were getting more help from teachers and teacher aides for individualized attention where needed. One white girl said, "I try to make friends and what happens? I get punched in the stomach." A white boy said sometimes the black boys gang up on him, and a black boy explained: "You see, many black kids act that way because they've been—what do you call it—frustrated for so long."

Mostly, the students handle their troubles themselves. I know case after case of this. For example, one white boy, a sixth grader who was a member of last year's Intergroup Council, found himself shut out by a black group after school on the playground. He came home earlier than his mother had expected—walked instead of waiting for the bus. When his mother asked him why, he told her but said he knew this would happen sometimes, it would change, probably next time they would let him join their play. He knew, from our many discussions in the council last year, that blacks have been shut out so long that it is only natural some will repeat the process with the whites.

Every child needs a place to shine. Our integrated schools must make sure every child has that place. An example is the experience of two sixth grade boys. In reading class, the black boy was having a hard time keeping up with the group. Although he received individual attention from the teacher, he also was helped by his white friend, an expert reader. Paired off in the new science program (developed cooperatively by the University of California at Berkeley and the district staff), it is the black boy whose skill and creativity emerged. The boys, as with other children, sat together at a small table experimenting with a kit of materials—wire and bulbs, battery, and a lump of clay. The black boy deftly hooked up the electrical equipment, then fashioned from the clay what the pair called "The Modern Statue of Liberty." He even lit her up. The white boy was so stimulated by this experiment that he went home and set up his own laboratory. His parents reminded him of his garden chores. Soon an arrangement was made to bring his black friend up to share the chores, then the boys would work together in the white boy's lab.

Another day, as I was walking through the cafeteria of one of the grades 4-6 schools after lunch, I saw the principal talking with a group of five girls—four black, one Mexican-American. With his nod of permission, I sat at a little distance and listened. This principal, a genius at handling "hard core" kids, grew up in poverty in a tough lumber town. He now shares his home with four foster teenage boys, as he has done for a number of years, and helps them develop into successful adults. He is so good with troubled children that they say kids get into trouble just to have a chance to talk with him. The five girls had been making it so hard for their white teacher that they were about to be suspended. They thought she was a bigot. She is not but she lacks experience with black children and perhaps she lacks some sensitivity, but she is learning.

"Listen, ladies, why do I take time to talk to you?" I heard the principal say. "Because I like you. You don't like me because I'm white. You hate my guts, but I can't help it that I'm white. I think you hate white people. Do you hate them because you think you're not as good as they are? What makes you think that? I think you're great, except for the way you've been acting."

The girls vociferously defended their action, blamed the teacher. Then, as the principal talked on, they dropped their heads and sat sullen. "Listen," said the principal. "Lift up your heads. I want you to stand tall."

Finally one said, "O.K., I can stand tall. I'm going to stand as tall as this school!" A week later, the principal told me, he got a note from one of the girls. "I used to hate your guts," she wrote. "But I don't anymore."

The girls' teacher, undoubtedly, was in part to blame. It is impossible to staff our schools totally with the kind of teachers we need for integration. The majority are doing an excellent job. Only a few fall down. In one school, a white teacher, who was outstandingly successful in his previous white school, is finding his new role painful. His students feel insecure, bored and restless. A few went to talk to a counselor about the problem. "We don't like him," they said and he answered, "Well maybe he thinks you don't like him." The group mulled that over, decided they'd try to show him they liked him. So one day they brought cakes and cookies and ice cream and gave him a surprise party. Things went better after that.

The principal of that school tells me he has four teachers who are not able to deal successfully with their classes —only four out of 32. Hopefully they can be helped to change. The fighting will diminish as the frustration ends. But I say over and over again these problems are a small price to pay for the gains we are making. Social gains have already been impressive. The achievement level, we know from our pilot busing of black children that began in 1966, will rise for the black children and will not decline for the white children. This we will not be able to measure conclusively for the next several years. We will be evaluating progress as we go on.

Some informal evaluations of the first 6 months of integration were reported to me in April, 1969, and I read them with pleasure at my desk in Boston. A glimpse, superficial but telling, was given by a San Francisco television reporter: "If the dozen parents I talked with reflect the situation, then the Berkeley program in this first six months hasn't lived up to either their fears or expectations. But those who were fearful, or opposed before integration began, say that things are working out better than they thought. Aside from integration, they want a good school for their children, and many of them are working to make it better."

A fantastic number of volunteers are working in the schools, they tell me. One school alone has 40. They are School Resource Volunteers, who register with that district organization, and parents who come in on their own. (The School Resource Volunteers number approximately 500.) Among them, as the television reporter said, are many white parents who feared the effect of integration on their children's achievement, and now here they are helping black children learn to read or write or do arithmetic.

A panel of principals reporting to the board, and the reports to the Director of Elementary Education from which they drew their comments, unanimously stressed the dedication of the teachers. Like the Intergroup Youth Council, they found friction diminishing, black-white friendships increasing, and the children working out problems by themselves in a realistic process. "The children are beautiful!" one principal exclaimed.

I think we must have a new definition of education.

Many of Berkeley's white parents in this highly intellectual community have been overly reliant on grades as a measure of their children's educational progress. I say grades, and what they measure, are only one thing. Education is a total venture which includes learning to know and face the world the way it is—black and white, all races and colors, learning to be a total human being in the real world.

Jim Wood, of the *San Francisco Examiner*, wrote a beautiful story about integration in November, 1968, integration's third month. He cited all the things that are happening, good and bad. And he came through with a story headed, "Berkeley Gets an 'A' in Integration."

I give it an A too, and invite other troubled cities to consider our plan. Here are the guidelines we found essential.

Encourage minority groups, especially the poor, to take the initiative. Support their courage in speaking out. They know what they need, what they are entitled to. Let them tell you. Bring out leaders of minority groups.

Elect Board of Education members willing to act boldly *in the interests of the total community.*

Select the kind of superintendent that a board wants— one committed to integrated, quality education, and one experienced in bringing it into action.

Involve the total staff—every teacher—in all decisions. Today's administrator cannot make decisions alone. Today's staff insists on helping him shape policy. This is fine. It's more work, but the result is great. Individuals and groups accept decisions they help make.

Involve all civic, university, church, business and service groups, and minority organizations from right to left. Include the Black Power leaders.

Listen to the reactionaries and fanatics but ignore their threats. . . .

Involve the parents every step of the way. Especially bring the minority parents into the schools, into the meetings, into the dialogue.

Tell the public what you're doing, thinking, planning. Keep the administrators' doors open. *Communicate*—professionally, through publicity, speeches, publications; personally, through contact with all community groups and agencies. Provide the public *with a calendar of what's ahead— then stick to your schedule.*

Stress *quality education for all.* Quality Education is Integrated Education. Make it possible for every child to achieve at his highest ability.

Hire teachers committed to all children. Screen them for prejudice. Initiate or join movements to make credentialing more flexible. Let promising teacher-trainees earn their credentials while teaching for pay. Pay them proper salaries.

Hire as many qualified minority group teachers—Negro, Oriental, Mexican-American—as you can get. Encourage minorities to enter teacher-training.

Revise the curriculum to *hit hard at Negro History.* Use textbooks that tell the truth and tell it in language understandable by the ghetto resident. If you can't find them, make your own. Develop Negro History units from preschool through elementary grades. Make sure it's an integral part of American History in the upper grades.

Provide Intergroup Education in-service units and seminars for the public as well. *Encourage staff involvement* in this crucial area of education.

Retrain the staff for a *new teaching style,* not in the old pattern of after-school courses but in released time. Release teachers for a month or two for retraining by hired experts and innovators.

Last, but far from least, draw on all available funds—local, state, federal and foundation. Quality public education costs money, integrated public education costs money, and quality integrated education is worth a great price. "We are rich enough to do what is necessary," and integration is not only necessary—it is crucial, if our democratic society is to live.

If we are going to prove that the plan works, we have more work to do. And we've got to prove it to the nation—to the doubters in high places, to the black separatists, to the fearful whites. What other cities will do depends largely on our success. We are continuing and expanding the efforts we made during last year's preparation to make integration work socially.

- We schedule social events—picnics and weekend retreats for both blacks and whites.
- We tie in after-school recreational programs to bring youngsters of different ethnic groups together in a play situation.
- We have hired 250 neighborhood aides to assist credentialed teachers in the integrated classrooms with behavior problems.
- We encourage black and Caucasian youngsters to visit one another's homes.
- We give sensitivity training to teachers and school officials —equipping them to cope with racial tensions and underlying prejudices.
- We involve the district's students, parents, and teachers in interracial workshops, meetings and neighborhood discussions.

We have overhauled our curriculum intensively and innovatively. We are using methods gleaned from massive cooperative study, and we are experimenting with methods never used before. So far, most parents have been supportive. The black community, in spite of those black separatists—as yet a minority—who currently tolerate integration as something "that will work for a while," is almost solidly back of us. Principals have added more individualized teaching, more music, more art by expanding teaching staff or teaching aides, by more team-teaching to meet the needs of children who were bored, and who were not finding the classroom program as rich and stimulating as it had been in the previous hill school. We have listened and we have acted.

The impact of my resignation, which I announced the day after integration began, to become, in February, 1969, Commissioner of Education for the Commonwealth of Massachusetts, has had a two-fold impact. The important one I witness is a rallying and heightening of support for integration. The general feeling was expressed: "We all worked with Sullivan—board, staff, teachers' organizations, parents—to achieve this. We shall see it through."

The other reaction, which I of course anticipated, comes from our old opponents, for whom I am now a sitting duck. They blasted me at board meetings, in the local press, and in daily stacks of letters that range from literate scorn to almost illegible profanity. "Sullivan," they say, "has made a national figure of himself at the expense of Berkeley taxpayers." They scream about the fantastic cost of this busing. They proclaim that many families have moved or are moving from Berkeley because of integration. The local newspaper plays up all the anti-integration, anti-Sullivan gripes. The other day they even printed one angry man's letter twice!

Yes, I get tired of the calumny. But I say again and

again, no change can be made without cost. Integration is worth the price. You decide to do it, and then you DO IT. You make the decision, as Martin Luther King declared— and as I shall continue to try to follow—"not because it is safe, or politic, or popular. You make it because it is right."

I look ahead with confidence that the promises I made will be kept—that all schools will remain integrated and that all vestiges of separate and unequal education in Berkeley will be removed.

As I conclude this chapter of the Berkeley story, I must think again of the man who motivated and challenged me to enter the fight to integrate our schools—who brought me to Prince Edward County and urged me to accept a position in a northern city where large numbers of Negroes lived. My dear friend Robert Kennedy. I remember the tragic days following the assassination of John F. Kennedy, when I visited his brother and encouraged him to remain active in public affairs. Robert Kennedy made his first public appearance after his brother's death in Prince Edward County in late spring 1964. The trip did much to restore his confidence. The children fell in love with him, and it was obvious that they gave him the psychological lift he so badly needed. One little girl handed him a note which read, "President Lincoln freed the slaves, President Kennedy freed the Negroes."

A few weeks later I was with him in the chambers of the Supreme Court of the United States when the court ended, once and for all, the Prince Edward story that had started ten years earlier in a companion case to *Brown vs. the Board of Education.*

During my years here in Berkeley I remained close to Robert Kennedy and Edward Kennedy. The late Senator took great pride in the work being done in the Berkeley public schools and urged other school systems to follow the Berkeley lead.

During the presidential primary campaign conducted here in California in the spring of 1967, I openly supported Robert Kennedy. The *Berkeley Gazette* sharply criticized my participation. "It is highly unethical for any appointed public official to enter the political arena," they editorialized. "It is a long established and well grounded unwritten law, that public officials appointed by elected officials remain silent on partisan politics—particularly on candidates for election. By observing this practice appointed officials avoid entering the gray area of confusing the public good with personal gain."

But the board backed me up, fulfilling its promise when I accepted the Berkeley superintendency that I could speak out on controversial matters. And Marc Monheimer, who was head of our School Master Plan Committee, wrote me his support, and sent a copy to the *Berkeley Gazette.*

[I] congratulate you upon taking a public position in support of Senator Robert Kennedy. The safe and easy course for any appointed public official is to avoid partisan comment and commitment. Perhaps that is the basic weakness in our system of administration of public affairs.

The law of California expressly permits school district employees to engage in political activity, subject to certain appropriate restrictions, and thereby encourages them to fulfill their role as citizens in a participatory democracy. For public employees to speak out on vital issues and in support of candidates for elective office requires far more courage than is required for them to remain silent. Your bold, courageous action will assist immeasurably in bringing to the attention of the community the views and opinions of our highly-trained and knowledgeable public servants concerning the really vital issues of this frightening and challenging age in which we live.

I was grateful for the support. I believed Robert Kennedy would fight for equal educational opportunities, and I was compelled to give him whatever help I could.

It is ironic that two of three gallant men who fought for equal rights wrote forewords for my two books on school integration—Robert F. Kennedy wrote the foreword for *Bound for Freedom* and Martin Luther King, the foreword for this book.

But if these men's lives, and their violent deaths, say anything else to us, they say that we must continue their struggles. Integration did not die with John Kennedy, or with Robert Kennedy, or with Martin Luther King. It lives, it will grow, and it will enrich this world in which we struggle. But we must do it now. We must "make real the promise of democracy." Now is the time.